2nd Annual Queen Lili'uokalani
Long Distance Canoe Races
September 3 & 4, 1994
Kailua-Kona, Hawaii

There is no, one, best way
to reach the peak, rather
there are many paths that
climb in different directions,
which all lead to the mountain top.
Immanuel Kant see a forest for da trees.
Rolling a rock thru a mist,
oui missed the myth of sisyfus...
but I'm practically over the hill, so chill!

3

Rabbit Droppings

A K A

Autobiography of a Wabbit:

the offbeat poetry, humor & memoirs of a baby boomer

by

Harvey T. Rabbit

*"that quality which appeals
to a sense of the ludicrous,
absurdly incongruous, or
comical & amusing"*

PUBLISHED BY
Rabbit Enterprises
West Roxbury, MA USA

Rabbit Droppings:
AKA
Autobiography of a Wabbit
by Harvey T. Rabbit

Published by
Rabbit Enterprises
359 Corey Street,
West Roxbury, MA 02132 USA

www.RabbitEnterprises.US
email: HTRabbit@aol.com
tel: Toll free: 1-866-263-3983 + PIN# 5320

Book & Cover Design & Book Layout by Nancy Kellerman
and Arrow Graphics, Inc.

ISBN : 0-9729059-0-1
Library of Congress Control Number: 2003091061

Rounded gray boxes indicates Internet Humor

Rabbit Droppings

In Memory of
Louis Yaloff,
Janis Ruth Coulter,
Joel Wallerstein,
and Ronny Silverman,
My uncle & three old friends,
all of whom died before their time.

I dedicate **Rabbit Droppings**, with profound
thanks and love, to my mother and brother,
and with special thanks to:
BVM, AA, JP, CF, BF, NM, NG, DH, JM, HB, SS,
J & MG, Liz, GC, SRJ, DHJ, EM, JSA, SK, and Wendell.

A Vietnam Vet still singin' the blues

written in 1993 ... by Alita Corcos

Harvey didn't come home from Vietnam with a purple heart. He came home with a speeding ticket! *"Driving thru the village a coupla times, I got shot at. Out of no where a bullet goes by your head, you don't know where it's coming from."* It was in this same area on a quiet day that he let the speedometer inch upwards. He was eager to get by without incident & unscathed, when the Military Police pulled him over for going 23 mph in a 15 mph zone.

Although he no longer worries about gunplay on his way to work, the effects of his experience in Vietnam still haunt him today. Harvey was never in the thick of combat. He was never forced to take another's life. But despite this relative good fortune, he suffers to this day from his experiences at war. *"The effects of Vietnam were delayed for me, but they caused a lot of problems."*

At a glance, Harvey doesn't look as if he has any more problems than the rest of us. He is tall, with a salt & pepper beard, and clear blue eyes. His first love is music. Harvey doesn't cringe at his memories of Vietnam. In fact he does the exact opposite. From happenings in Boot Camp to accidental death in the compound, Harvey's stories about Vietnam run the gamut from extraordinary to repulsive. Harvey delights in such colorful stories, and his energetic storytelling style guarantees a reaction from his listener. It's obvious that his personality didn't suffer from being in Vietnam. However, difficulties in working with and relating to people are a reality he confronts daily.

When Harvey worked as a media specialist in 1993 at BU's Sargent College of Allied Health Professions, his supervisor, Lucia, said: "Inherently, Harvey is a sweet guy, & he's sincere in wanting to do a good job, but Harvey gets anxious about his job, and I have to tell him, calm down, there's always tomorrow."

This type of anxiety is typical for Vietnam Veterans. A 1983 Congressional study was launched to *"establish the prevalence & incidence of Post-Traumatic Stress Disorder (PTSD) and other psychological problems in readjusting to civilian life among Vietnam Veterans."* The study found Vietnam Veterans suffer from a range of symptoms, including recurring thoughts and nightmares about particular events, irritability, outbursts of anger, difficulty concentrating & difficulty falling or staying asleep.

Harvey was never officially diagnosed with PTSD, even though he spent a total of two years in Veteran's Administration Hospitals during the late 70's early 80's. *"Harvey has made tremendous progress,"* his mother said.

He still has difficulty concentrating, though. *"Some of the recreational activities in Vietnam may be to blame for these traits as well."*

Harvey received his Honorable Discharge from the Marines in the early 70's & returned home to Boston. Then he tossed around, first the US & afterwards the world, searching for his niche. He *"decided to go to California to seek fame & fortune so I got my cat, Kitty, and we split for the Coast but she ran away from me on New Buffalo Commune in Taos, New Mexico."*

Harvey couldn't find a job in California & he ended up wandering around the campus of U.C. @ Berkeley right after the Yom Kippur War where a booth was set up on the lawn soliciting volunteers for Israel. Harvey turned around, drove back to Boston and hopped a plane for a Kibbutz program in Israel where he met his long time friend, Naomi. *"Harvey & I are close friends, almost like family. He's very generous and gets a lot of self esteem from helping other people. Harvey is an outgoing, humorous, and sensitive person. Music is a very big part of his life. He also writes poetry. Have you ever read any of his poetry?"*

Rainy day #2

anyway I iz blue
but lets sing shoo-bee-doo
then we'll change & in lieu
of blue – we'll be orange ya glad
dat chu knew – who she do?

    rainy daze numero tree, wood ya pleas
    do you see what I saw – aw(pshaw)
    Where's da poor? on the shore?
    whilst oui snore like a whore,
    who is bored to the core –
    & what for?
    We deplore lousy war!

Rabid rabbit drop-ins

The story of a hairy hare who's barely here,
not there, but bears fears, & cares for dears –
butt where's maiden fairs? da news:

Dr. Seuss (silly goose) was loose,
had a ruse with a moose of no use
& a truce wit Lenny Bruce's
papoose's caboose.

Is an electric train refrain from SANE, or watt?

....

"Harvey" was an old movie with Jimmy Stewart about a guy named Elwood P. Dowd, who had a friend named Harvey, who was a 6-foot invisible rabbit (Pooka).

PORTRAIT OF HARVEY T.

by one rapidly, rabbinic, recurringly rabid, rabbit, repetitively raving, regarding relevant voltage, really redundant, electric or watt? Darned draining, knit picking, yarn spinning, thread weaving, knot too mention tying me bucko up the shaft, screwed up aft! or is dat daft? Too true, Nu, yu?

Childhood 1950-60

I was born in Mattapan, Massachusetts on February 8, 1950 (Aquarius) to Jean & Morris, and don't remember much about my early years. When I was a baby, my father called the old neighbor lady downstairs a KaKa! Then I recall a scene with my brother, Dick, pulling me in a sled with a baby seat, down Harvard Street in the snow! The next memories I have are "walking the plank" from the moving truck over the front stairs into our new home in West Roxbury...then I remember my Mom bringing home a puppy (1/2 german shepherd & 1/2 beagle – a mutt we named Lucky), taking him downstairs to the basement to put him in a box. He was a mongrel who liked to chase cars & dig thru garbage cans. After several years, My Mom had Lucky put to sleep because he threw up on the living room rug, after eating grass...It took me 3 days to realize that he was missing & I was heartbroken when I found out!

My whole family used to go to the beach at Wingaersheek in Gloucester most every Sunday during the summer – I loved it! We have several pictures of me, playing with my brother & sister, digging a huge hole, about 5 or 6 feet in diameter, & 5 feet deep.

One time I was walking home from my nearby elementary school, the Patrick F. Lyndon, when I found a dollar bill on the street – in 1960, I was in heaven. I stopped at the Penny Candy Store to buy 19 packs of baseball cards, each with a free bubble gum in it plus a candy bar – all a nickel a piece. Now I had a collection of baseball cards like all the other kids!

I had two neighbors that I was very friendly with, Alan & Susan. We used to "play Doctor" (you show me yours, I'll show you mine). But we were about 10 or 11 & nobody was very developed physically.

Hare Jews

Then there's the time when I was in the 6th grade at the P. F. Lyndon School, with our teacher, Mr. Donahue – a very tall man who seemed to loom over the whole classroom! He gave us an assignment to take turns giving talks in front of the class. The girls were to talk about bicycles while the boys were supposed to talk about hair do's! However, I've always had a little hearing or understanding problem & I heard "hair juice"! I didn't quite know what "hair juice" was, but I was determined to improvise. So I got up in front of the class at the same time as the girl (we were both supposed to talk at once to see who could hold the interest of the class). Well I was off: "Hair juice comes in 5 delicious colors & flavors…" I started babbling on & on about the merits of hair juice. The girl & the rest of the class were dumbfounded! Eventually, the teacher asked: "What the heck are you talkin' about?" "Hair Juice," I proclaimed. "No", he said, "hair do's, dummy!"

If electricity comes from electrons…does that mean that morality comes from morons?

If lawyers are disbarred and clergymen defrocked, doesn't it follow that electricians can be delighted, musicians denoted, cowboys deranged, models deposed, tree surgeons debarked, and dry cleaners depressed?

HIGH SCHOOL 1961–67

Boston Latin School (BLS)

I took piano lessons at 9 for 1 year from Fay C., an old maid Italian lady who lived down the street from me & who was very friendly but my Mom stopped the lessons when I wasn't practicing regularly. I also took acoustic bass lessons for 1 year in 7th grade at BLS. I took 'bone lessons for 1 year in 8th grade & bought a Holton Collegiate trombone from Mr. Young, the band leader, for $150 in 1962. Then I continued taking 'bone lessons from John Coffee for several years in his store across from Symphony Hall. Mr. Coffee would have me bring my horn into his office where we would sit next to each other in front of his desk with a stand of Arban's Exercises. He had a big ashtray with a cigarette going constantly even when he played along! But he was an oldtimer who really got around; he played in the Boston Symphony with Koussavitsky!

I played in the BLS orchestra, marching band & jazz band, was a participant in Jr. Achievement, & was elected President of my "company"— we made 1st aid kits & hanger/yarn dusters. I rowed in crew at BLS in 1966 & '67 on the Charles River and danced in regional USY Israeli dance competitions (1963–'67) called Shirekudia & we won!

I spent senior year summer working at Capitol warehouse in South Boston on C St. (days) with an Italian guy named Salvi & our supervisor Joe. What a crew. We goofed off a lot, but always got our work done. It was a grocery warehouse, where we transferred produce every morning to the different market locations & put up grocery orders for the stores. Nights & weekends, I went down to Kenburma Street at Nantasket Beach in Hull with a group of my buddies. We had many adventures there.

My 1st job was working as a porter at the Cheri theater complex in 1966. I smoked my 1st joint "up on the roof" with a cute fellow employee.

WOODSTOCK – AUG. 1969

While on leave from Camp Pendleton, California, I went home where my friends bought me a ticket for a 3 day concert: Woodstock! We drove in 2 car loads. My buddy, Dave, who was on crutches, drove one of the cars. We left at 6PM on Fri nite & got to the median strip, 12 miles from the concert site at the highway exit for Beth-El, N.Y., at 6 in the morning on Sat. We hitch-hiked the last 12 miles, riding both in & "on" slow moving cars that were allowed to proceed, cuz when we got there, the exit was closed to further traffic! So we hopped on & off, in & outa cars all along the way, stopping to speed & trip with other friendly, hip, people of both sexes. At one point I had a sign that read SPEED on 1 side & ACID on the other. We finally arrived at the hill overlooking the concert site at midnite on Sat. nite when Janis Joplin, Big Brother & da Holdin' company were on. I also saw Jimi Hendrix play the Star Speckled Bannana at dawn!

Q: If you cross LSD with birth control pills,
 do you win a trip without the kids?

Q: If you take an Oriental person and
 spin them around several times,
 do they become disoriented?

Q: Did you hear about the Indian chief named Running Water?
 He had two daughters, Hot and Cold,
 and a son named Luke.

Practice safe eating, always use condiments.

**Condoms should be used on
every conceivable occasion.**

I fired my masseuse today. She just rubbed me the wrong way.

USMC BOOT CAMP – JAN 69

Jeff Parent, a friend from UMASS, went to Vietnam in the Marines & got killed. After that, I got alienated, decided to drop out of school & enlist in the Marine Corps! I also volunteered for Vietnam, leaving for Boot Camp by train from Boston to Parris Island, South Carolina on 6 JAN 69. When I arrived, there was a bus to take us to the Marine Base. When we got off the bus, they took everything from us and herded us into a barracks to sleep for the nite. The next morning, bright & early, they took us in for our "haircuts". A little off the top meant shave my head like a jarhead! Then we got our military clothes in a mish mash until we had all our gear in a duffel bag which we were required to lug around for a while until we got our assignments for platoons. All the while, Drill Sergeants were barking out furious orders to run here & there, do this & that, etc.

When we came out of the mess hall one day, the D.I.'s (Drill Instructors) got us back to the barracks, and announced: *"Who spit on my Parade Deck, ladies?"* You could hear a pin drop – nobody breathed a word. Finally one D.I. went up to a guy named Grabowski & said, *"You did it, you puke, didn't you?"* Grabowski denied it for a while but the D.I. knew the truth. He finally admitted it & broke down sobbing. The D.I. cleared his throat and hucked a thick lugee of phlegm on the floor and said *"Lick it up!"* Believe it or not, that kid licked up that crap! Yuk I would have had the shit kicked out of me before I would do that!

Then there was the time a guy cheated at the rifle range during qualification week so the D.I.'s literally kicked him from one end of the squadbay to the other, beating the crap out of him in the process. When he protested that he would "write his congressman," the D.I.'s said, *"Anybody see anything, ladies? No, Sir"* we all rang out. The fear & intimidation were immense and universal! He was not allowed to sit for the rest of qualification week, which was no small thing since he even had to stand for meals & classes. He was only allowed to rest for 6 or less hours a night, when he went to sleep.

Infantry Training Regiment & Supply School-Camp LeJeune, N.C.

April & May 1969

When I went to advanced infantry training, that everyone was required to take, I was doing OK for a while then we went on field maneuvers & were back at a perimeter camp where we were grabbing a meal at the mess. We had to eat on trays outside on long high metal grill like tables with no chairs (we had to stand) so we were putting the trays of food on the table but someone from another company which was in rivalry with my company hung his M16 Rifle between the grill where the trays were (which he was definitely not supposed to do! You're supposed to keep your rifle on your person at all times in the field except to sleep).

I picked up a canteen cup full of milk I was drinking & inadvertently spilled some milk on this guy's rifle – well he flipped out and grabbed the rifle, attacking me! However, I was in full battle gear (a flak jacket & helmet)! Two of his buddies followed his lead and also jabbed at me with their rifles. Well, when my buddies saw this, a huge rumble ensued. However, one of the guys had rifle butted me in the eyebrow on my forehead & I was bleeding, so (although I was tremendously hungry), I had to leave my whole tray without touching a bite except for a sip of milk which started the whole ruckus! I walked calmly away to the medical tent while all hell broke loose around me. I was treated and sent back to the rear out of the field maneuvers for a few days to recover while the ver-kak-tah fighting flamed on.

The next day, I was walking down the street of the base with a big bandage on my eye when the Commanding General of the base drove by and saw me. He stopped to ask me what had happened, so after I told him, he said he would have an officer interview me to court martial the other guys who had attacked me & that is, in fact, what happened!

5th Force Service Regiment,

Camp Pendleton, California – July '69

1969, after boot camp, advanced ITR & supply school, I was stationed in Oceanside, California, at 5th FSR, Camp Pendleton. I was a PFC and worked as a supply administration clerk. My sister lived in LA (Culver City) at the time, & I used to hitch-hike up the coast every weekend to visit.

One time I went up & hung out with a teenage neighbor of my sister's. The teenager & her friend got me to take some psilocybin (a chemical derivative of mescaline, a hallucinogenic drug similar to acid – LSD). I was fine while I was hanging in the back of someone's van for the drive-in movie. I missed it, but never mind, I was tripping quite nicely, then everybody went home and they dropped me off at my sister's apt., but she was away for the night, so I went in by myself and started to have a bummer.

I was lying down listening to Inna-Gadda-Davida and time seemed to be moving at an incredible rate. I looked at my watch and the hour hand was moving as fast as the second hand, etc. I was really freaking out so I went out into the courtyard and saw the neighboring apt. where I knew the teenage girl, but it was now 3 AM. I went over and tried their door. It was open so I went in & entered the parents' bedroom where the husband sat up immediately, and I said "Is Karen home"? They were dumbfounded but said nothing, so I walked out and freaked out further – walking down the street and eventually deciding that I was no good and needed to die so I lay down in the middle of the street, but it was a side street so no traffic came, plus it was 5 AM, on a weekend so I eventually got up and went back to my sisters apartment – this too shall pass.

USMC 1969-70

So I got alienated at UMASS in Amherst, dropped out of school, enlisted in the USMC, got stationed in California and wanted to go to Vietnam. I requested a transfer thru the regular channels but they claimed my MOS (job specialty) was critical and thus I would need to be replaced with someone who needed to be trained in supply administration school, and was refused. So in exasperation I wrote to my Congressmen and Senator Ted Kennedy came thru for me – I had orders for 'Nam in a month. Here's a copy of that letter:

July 8, 1969
H&S Co. H&S Bn.
5th FSR, (-)FMF
Camp Pendleton, CA 92055

Dear Senator Kennedy:

I am a resident of Boston, Massachusetts in the Marine Corps. I have requested to be sent to RVN (Vietnam) & have been turned down because my Military Occupational Specialty (MOS) is supposed to be critical. I am in the supply field (MOS-3041) There are new Marines constantly coming out of supply school going into this field.

I joined the Marine Corps to mature and try to decide what I want to do for my life's work. I went to the University of Massachusetts for a year and a half and then dropped out because I found myself not studying & felt I wasn't ready to attend college. I felt that 2 years away from everything would make me think and also mature to the point where I would be able to decide upon a major in college when I returned. I felt service in Vietnam would especially make me re-evaluate myself & my life ambitions.

So it is very important for me to serve in Vietnam. It seems ironic that there are so many youths in the country today who refuse to go in the military for fear of being sent to Vietnam and at the same time there are servicemen who want to go to Vietnam & can not because their requests are refused. I ask you very sincerely if there is anything you can do to help me get sent to Vietnam. I would greatly appreciate any help you can provide.

Sincerely yours,
HTRabbit, PFC USMC

11th Motor Transport Battalion–1st MarDiv RVN

Jan–Dec/1970

I arrived in country after going thru prep. at Camp Pendleton (in Oceanside, CA). Again, I was stationed in a supply office, where I held down 3 different jobs: requisition clerk, fiscal clerk, & jeep driver. I picked up rank (Sgt. E-5) quickly, because I kept my nose clean & stayed out of trouble... for a while. I was very unhappy at first because I didn't like the Enlisted Club–I wasn't much of a drinker. Heck, I didn't even like the taste of beer, didn't drink hard liquor yet, so eventually someone turned me onto "herb". It was great–we bought a bag of 50 pre-rolled joints (of the best quality), in exchange for a carton of cigarettes (for which we paid $1.50 at the PX), so we were paying 3 cents a joint, not bad! Plus we used to get this gooey opium and coat the joints making them into superstuff–WOW!

Then I had the duty of "burning the shitters!" We had outhouses comprised of huts with 4 wooden seats with holes under which we placed 1/2's of 55 gal drums filled with diesel fuel into which everyone shat! Then, every morning, someone had the duty of dragging these 1/2's of 55 gal. drums filled with diesel fuel & shit, out of the outhouses, lighting them up into thick, putrid, black, smoke pouring out onto the countryside.

I picked up rank quickly and before long I was a Sgt. (E-5), an NCO (Non Commissioned Officer). However, I stayed friendly with my lower ranking friends and eventually got written up on charges of fraternization with the troops and dereliction of duty (which was a trumped up charge, and totally untrue). I requested a transfer out of that outfit from the commanding officer of the Battalion. The Col. saw me, chewed me out, and asked if I was a quitter. I replied no, but I refused to accept untrue charges about my work and being friendly with the troops should not be a crime, especially in war time! He slapped my wrist and sent me back to the supply office.

The student who said his bible had been run over by a steamroller, was stretching the truth.

The judge dismissed the litigation involving a handbag made out of a sow's ear as being a trivial purse suit.

Clothes don't necessarily make the man, but a good suit makes a lawyer.

Circular arguments often make the rounds.

Do Lipton Tea employees take coffee breaks?

Why she dares assume airs
boo coo pairs splitting hairs,
from such dares, lawyers' heirs
grind their gears, it appears
I've got bills in arrears
seems I'z years fighting fears,
watching bears killing deers,
drinking beers, shedding tears,
sensing death as it nears.
Is there anyone who cares?

Here's a satirical letter I wrote while working in a Marine Corps supply office in Danang, Vietnam.

Office of the Fahrquar
Peripherastic & Alamachaz Unit
1st Force Recon. Patrol Company
Camp Farthington on the Moor
Santa Sal Syringe,
Plungeville Plantation
Occa-lumba-chumba,
S.C.L.L.L.L./LLL/LL/L/Ricky Recon
69 JUN 1969

From: Commanding Ferquist
To: Private Ricky R. Recon
Via: CMC, CG MCB CAMPEN, CG MCB CLNC,
       CG 5th MARDIV (FMF PAC), PFC U.R.A TURD
Subj: Reference (a), (b), (c)
Ref: (a) Intercervical communicative processes concerning
           defecation.
       (b) Feroxive Directives FDO 6900.69 S
       (c) Fornication

1. It has come to the attention of this office that carnal knowledge in accordance with reference (c) is deficient according to reference (b).
2. By means of ref. (a), you are hereby directed to submit a report in accordance with ref. (b) concerning the practice of ref. (c).
3. This report will be submitted no later than Julian date 9669-0000 to this office. A negative report is required.
4. Private Ricky R. Recon is hereby relieved of all duties & responsibilities as Assistant Fahrqueer for the 6th Fahral District. Pvt. Recon is assigned to the 9th Force Recon Force & is hereby forced to use force on any forces resisting force. Any person resisting Reference (c) according to reference (b) as directed by reference (a), will be on report to the 1st Fahrquart Assisting Reconnaissance Tarts (1st F.A.R.T). The 1st F.A.R.T. will put such offenders up for admonishment according to FCO 96.69 S-69 and the responsible Fahrqueert in charge will use sublimation to guide such addenders towards the proper goals of Fahrquility & Fahrquist for all.

Last Lieutenant Lewis L. LuLu Loonie, Jr.
Division Rear (By subtraction)

After being introduced to Marijuana, about the 1st month in country, I stayed high constantly with a group of other "heads". We would get up in the morning, smoke a joint, then go to formation at 7 AM, smoke another joint before breakfast, go to work and, you guessed it, a coffee break to smoke more herb. Then we went back to work until lunch (after which we smoked again), returned to work for the afternoon until another "coffee break". We'd work till supper & more herb, work after supper for an hour, then smoke all evening till bed. This was our daily schedule, except when we had to stay up all night for guard duty.

I was Sgt of the Reactionary Squad which would be able to "react" to any emergency situation (2 people on a watch) for 5 or was it 6 – two hour shifts, roaming around the compound with a radio and reporting in, every hour. However, things were usually pretty quiet, so I assigned the "heads" the watches late at night/early morning & I walked around with them, smoking herb all nite & drinking a half bottle of OBESITOL, a cough medicine bottle of diet stuff (a tablespoon a day to lose weight) but we used 1/2 a bottle and 7 joints to stay up all night.

One time the TOP SGT. put 2 African American Marines in an old medical bunker and used it as a brig to keep the men on restriction from free movement, like jail but they had not been properly sentenced. I was instructed to place 2 men from the Reactionary Squad in front of the bunker and guard the prisoners, only allowing them to go to the bathroom, accompanied by a guard, and then right back to the med. bunker/Illegal brig; and I was also told not to allow more then 2 people at a time in front of the "brig". Well it turns out that the 2 "prisoners" were friends of mine who were "heads", So I put the guard/heads in charge of taking the prisoners to the bathroom and turning them on surreptitiously to some herb, then returning them to the bunker.

Well it was right after such a trip that the TOP SGT. wandered by and saw the aftermath of a guard change for the bunker when the 2 old guards were hanging out schmoozing with the 2 new guards and I was hanging out supervising all this schmoosing – 5 people in front of the med. bunker/"brig". The TOP SGT. freaked out and yelled to get away from the prisoners, etc. The next day I was called into the Company office and told that all 5 of us were being brought up on charges of neglecting prisoners, etc. or some such stupid thing, and would we accept Non Judicial Punishment from our Commanding Officer instead of a Court Martial? I refused, requested a Court Marshall, and advised all the others to do the same. They did, & the whole thing was dropped the next day cuz the lifers knew they were operating an illegal brig. It was after that, that I was brought up on those dereliction of duty charges.

Condescending: A prisoner escaping down the wall using a rope.

About a month before the end of my stay in country, we sent the supply truck out on a Sat. evening run to pick up a Vietnamese Hooker. The truck brought her into the compound for the night surreptitiously, and we hid her in the security cage, upstairs in the supply warehouse, where she proceeded to screw Marines all nite for pairs of Boots, C-Rations, cartons of cigarettes or $5 a throw (per trick) Then the truck made a "run" in the morning and took her home.

When I returned home to Massachusetts from Vietnam, I arranged to visit a girlfriend (Andrea Beth) in Providence at her family's home. She took me to see a popular movie that was playing at the time, LOVE STORY – well after seeing that and yearning for this girl the whole time I was in the service, I asked her to marry me. I was 21 and she was 19. She said "I don't know", which translates into NO and we eventually drifted apart!

HI, Y'all!

No meaning at all, (knot atol, high atop, hi ya pops goes da sea gull) not at all on the ball, I'd rather you call Monty Hall, Salty Sol, than to push (with such gall) paltry Paul, off that wall (oh so tall) down dat knoll, cuz he'd fall, maybe maul Lenny's moll (barbie doll), in the hall, then we'll haul U to court Mary Jane in da weeds, chewin' cheez, she procured siftin' seeds for da G's, buyin bee pollen, naturaleeze!

BYE, Y'all

Two Jewish men, Mr. Cohen and Mr. Abrahams, sit down in a smart kosher restaurant and a snooty waiter comes over to take their order. "Sirs, what can I get you?" inquires the waiter. "A glass of orange juice," says Mr. Cohen. "A glass of orange juice for me, too," says Mr Abrahams, but please make sure the glass is clean." The waiter stalks off in a disagreeable manner, and eventually comes back with two glasses of orange juice. "So," he says, "which one of you wanted the clean glass?"

"Chak mir nicht kein chinak" –
>> **Fig:** Don't bother me!
>> **Lit:** Don't knock my tea kettle (Sic)!
>> **HTR:** Don't hock my beer bottle (Hic)!

"Kish-mir in tochis"–
>> **Fig:** K.M.A.
>> **Lit:** kiss my rear end!
>> **HTR:** here's my nude friend!

Are you a Goy or are you a Jew? with your long curly hair — you look like a few dat I knew who were blue or could woo (or named Sue) — boo-hoo cried the dew! Ahoy Harvey Tea, rabidly rabbinic, rapidly reluctant, relatively redundant, revolving around rare, bit, care, butt, Rabbit juice: herbal essence!

watt iz dis electrifyin' Klezmer sound we hear all around? Dancing, joyous rhythms abound!

Attempts to filter all life's negatives
can get you high -ay- yay-yoy-oy-yoy, oh-boy!

Bluish hues, paying dues, abdicating booze, craving shmooze, no one lose — Oh you silly rabbit! Focus Habit, we'll have Nun of that.

What happened to the grey areas: READ grey matter deed between the lions will have you roaring on the floor in Stream of Consciousness...babble, scrabble, shake a tail feather, whether or knot wish we were together — who's Heather? No Way, Jose! I dunno, Bo, Bridges the gap, building seed money for tzedakah!

AM YISRAEL CHAI -wadda bout my why?
Is the opposite of meaning, kindly?
Is a poem, a song?
MEANING: rhyming, melodic rhythm,
oar is a boat, why is a lie, not (sew) high,
tie is a knot, true, the sky...(why) sigh iz to try, not to die,
π dat's arithmetic, mathematical cry, by the by...
A-THEMATIC Guy...
                    stowed aboard a boat,
oar a schism in the rowed!

When eye strain from peeling potatoes
feels caught in the web & flow
of onion flavored chocolate drops,
factory kisses lie apart from tears,
where I leers at affordable
shares of the blues dues plan.

Julius and Irving, two very religious Jewish men, visited Marcus Pinkus, the tailor, to have new black suits made. When they went to pick up the suits, Julius looked at his suit very carefully, held it up to the light, walked over to the window and examined it more carefully and then proclaimed, "Marcus, this suit is navy blue. It's not black!" "Trust me," said Marcus, "it's black!" "Irving, what do you think? Blue, or black?" asked Julius. "To tell you the truth," said Irving, "I couldn't really tell from this light if it's blue or black".

They left wearing their new suits and while walking down the street kept examining each other's suit to see if it was blue or black. Then they spotted two nuns standing on the corner and decided to go stand next to them. They knew their habits would be black and this way they could be sure.

Well, later that afternoon, the two nuns returned to the convent and visited with the Mother Superior to discuss their day in the city. "A very strange thing occurred," reported one of the nuns. "Two Jewish men approached us on the street and they were speaking Latin!" "Latin?" exclaimed Mother Superior. "Jewish men don't speak Latin; they speak Hebrew!" "No," said the other nun, "it was definitely Latin." "Well, what did they say exactly?" asked the Mother Superior. "I'm not really sure," said one of the nuns "They just kept repeating the same Latin phrase: 'Marcus Pinkus Fuctus!'"

Mix-a-lydian sound & meaning into a blend
of seething & breathing life into being
an offbeat poetic musingly musical
leaning towards the piece da resistance!

Absurd pity ditty:
aka path o' city insipidity
bip-ity, dip-ity, skip-ity, bop!
pity da poor, Pueblo re-bop
a-needle, scoobie doobie,
tweedle deedle, poodle noodle, bippity bop,
oodles of doodles, doin' dip-ity POP !

Insipidity, toodle-oodle, be-bop a noodle
to ewe, too Boo Beau! Few do! Coo Coo
(doze crazy pidgeons)flying fatefully from
derision, divining decision, milking it for all
tits worth, dairy, daily, vision: Moo Moo
on dee butt-her hand,
tits udderly diriculous!

Who knew da cue for hue of brew w/dew for ewe?
Watt do you do wit a sheepish grin?
Rosh Hashanah, elect-trick sin,
Yom Kippur, it's in...da season o' repentence,
where da yen fer zen, when, then, & again –
seized Big Ben's no-bull porpoise,
ducking da goose from abstruse abuse-wit.

We'll send her vender to lend her tender gender
and mend her fender bender, will it offend her?
Obtuse is loose from moose wit noose of no use.

INSIPIDITY strikes agin & again,
demand da men, da women, ten children plus
Minyan wit Bunyon pauls over my whammy,
Sammy Davis, Jr. Achievement, prize for Presley
leaping into Prez – it's happenin' – now's da thyme
for a spicy, saucy, herbal, mellow, fellow, not yellow,
jello, nor assinine butt Or-thello in bordello – Hello!

NUCLEAR + WARFARE
ECONOMIC POOR HERE
ENVIRONMENTAL NO CARE
DISREGARD OF WELFARE
BREED & POWER TRIP
PAIR A GORIC GHASTLY GREED GEAR! HUMAN JUSTICE
NO WHERE TO BE FOUND
THE EARTH BARE, TURN AROUND THE WORLD, DARE TO
BRAVE LIKE INDIAN BEAR THE BURDEN, SEED THE LAIR
OF SOULS WHO'D SHED A TEAR
FOR PEACE + LOVE + FREEDOM FAIR =
CHILDREN, THERE'S A REASON, CARE !
    ... pass the peas pleaz, goober's here.

(On going...)

Sad, silent, sadistic,
silly, salient, autistic,
jigolo jack horner,
sitting on 2nd curb, eating way,
spun ontological webs,
goading Gonzales to greater
& grandeur heights,
rite off ramp at JEROME on Pike
near Kitty Corner   <∞>   Ω   <∞>

> You never really learn to swear
> until you learn to drive.

UMASS & VISTA 1971–73

When I got out of the service I bought a sporty Buick Opel Cadet for $2000. It was a showroom model, with a black vinyl roof & a 4 speed on the floor! I went back to UMASS Amherst and during the summer I lived in a house in Hadley on Rte 9 with a barn & everything! There was only one other guy living there, who was also a DJ at WMUA (Umass college radio station), and we found a Swedish girl to move in for the summer. We were very liberated and all 3 of us took baths together. It was great fun-share water, ya grok?

Two ears tears, drip drop, flip plop, tic, tac, do, re, mi, kant chu, berryseed sprout wit out weed, groovin' high, flyin', sigh, must kneads dough ray of sun is one, too true blue, if knew, den iniquity wood stew da brew bubbling in lieu of boo-hoo ! Cries thru-out da Knight, fright from impending flight from fight for freedom.

**whoa... slow it down on the ground,
don't impound sound in da round,
unless dee symbols clash wit percussive
resounding vibrations. NONVIOLENT ones,
gestation, period!!!**

I joined VVAW (Vietnam Veterans Against the War) and demonstrated to close Westover Air Force base when Nixon mined Haiphong harbor in 1972. I lived at UMASS Amherst, Orchard Hill, in Webster house at that time, & took some residential college courses: first aid, & leathermaking. I also drove a Five College bus between Smith College in

Northampton, Amherst College, Hampshire College, Mt. Holyoke College, & UMASS – eventually I drove for the UMASS Transit Service in 1986.

Unfortunately my roommates at Swiss Village drove me to a nervous breakdown and I ended up at the VA Hospital in Northampton for 2 weeks on a locked ward. After quitting school and returning to the Boston University Continuing Education Program (BU-CEP), I volunteered for VISTA in 1973 and lasted about 6 months at Belchertown State School (Hospital), working as a Psych. Asst. with severely & profoundly retarded kids-adolescents. I started teaching a course sponsored by our boss at Belchertown (a progressive Psychiatrist/Psychologist named Jay Y.) and got 25 UMASS students to sign up for my 3 credit course entitled: Practicum in Mental Retardation which met one evening a week for 3 hours at Orchard Hill Residential College in the lounge. We had guest speakers every week, and the students had to do readings and come to Belchertown twice a week for 2 hours at a pop, spending one to one time with a resident, & consistently seeing the same person for the whole semester, building a relationship with that resident, and keeping a journal. I even had the sister of one resident in the course and actually got her brother to speak for the first time in years – very gratifying but kind of surprising. I don't know what I did to elicit his speech other than talking to him.

Eventually I started feeling very lonely and started going to the dayroom on my off hours to "observe the residents" by sitting in a rocking chair and silently rocking along with all the other patients.

After a while, I dropped out of the VISTA program and drove cross country with my cat, Kitty! We left for California with all my stuff in an Opel Kadett. I made it to New Orleans where I snuck Kitty Kat into a motel for the weekend while I went looking for company. I was walking thru the French Quarter at night and I finally picked up a girl who came back to my motel & slept with me. Turns out she was on the run from a convent. Later I found out she gave me the "crabs" – Brother! After that, I drove thru Texas. It took a day and a half with the only stop in a rest area to sleep for a few hours.

I made it to Taos, New Mexico, where I knew someone at a commune called New Buffalo. I slept in an open Adobe hut on the first nite with Kitty in my arms. Unfortunately, when I woke up, Kitty was nowhere to be found. So I stayed at the commune for 2 weeks looking for her and helping out around the place. I helped build a corral, but I had to finally leave for LA to see my sister, w/o Kitty. I left the cat food at the commune & told them to feed her if she ever showed up.

I arrived in LA & stayed with my sister in Culver City, getting a temp. job painting apartments at which I stunk! After 2 weeks, I decided to drive up the coast to San Francisco, where I found a year's waiting list for the fire department. I nixed the idea of joining the Coast Guard (after 2 years in the Marines, no thanks). So I arrived at the campus of UC Berkeley with no job & no place to sleep other than my car. I was discouraged to say the least! While wandering around the campus of UC Berkeley, I saw a table set up on the lawn seeking volunteers to go to Israel. (It was immediately after the Yom Kippur War), so I drove back to the East Coast, & arranged to go to Israel for a year starting with a Kibbutz Ulpan where I would learn to speak Hebrew fluently.

The winter of 1998-99 was tough on many of Europe's root crops. A week before Passover the Jewish Community of Madrid found that the shipment of horseradish it had ordered from Bolivia would now not arrive until ten days after the Passover ended. The community needed the horseradish for its traditional paschal ritual of Morror, but whoever they approached among the European suppliers, gave them the same reply: "Sorry! No can do."

In desperation, the Rabbi phoned one of his Yeshiva friends in Tel Aviv, and begged him to organize the dispatch of a crate of Israeli horseradish roots, by air-freight to Madrid. It took the friend a couple of days to organize, but two days before Passover, a crate of grade A tear-jerking Israeli horseradish roots was proudly loaded at Ben Gurion Airport onto the El-Al flight 789 destined for Madrid, Spain, and all seemed to be well.

Unfortunately, when the Rabbi came to Madrid Airport in order to take the crate out of Customs, he was informed that an unforeseen wildcat strike had just broken out among the members of the airport s Transport and General Workers Union after only a small amount had been off-loaded. He was heart sick to find out that no further shipments would be off-loaded for at least four days. So you see that's why "the chraine in Spain stayed mainly on the plane."

Don't pluck with harpists, fiddle with violinists, or anyone's beau!

ISRAEL 1973-74

I didn't realize about the crabs until months later when I was in Israel on Kibbutz Messilot, near Beit-Shan at Mt. Gilboa on the Jordan Border, where I was studying Hebrew 1/2 a day on an Ulpan, & working the other 1/2 of the day in the fish ponds, or in the lemon/orange/grapefruit orchards, or jumping up & down in wagons of cotton, or in the kitchen, in the dining hall, washing pots & pans, etc.

I had a young, perverted French roommate who had magazines with pictures of women doin' it with donkeys. He spoke no English & I spoke no French, so we quickly learned to communicate with each other in pidgin Hebrew. After only a week or so, we were going into town together for a drink where we met Moshe the con man, with whom I later became close friends until he died of lung cancer. Moshe preyed on middle-aged women, tourists with whom he would develop a close intimate relationship very quickly, & sweep them off their feet – often borrowing their money to pay for his wooing, entertaining, & showing the country to them. Everyone had a good time but there were undoubtedly many broken hearts.

On one occasion, I slept with a beautiful tall, thin Swedish girl, who was a volunteer on the Kibbutz. The next day she asked me how my neighbors "down south" were doing. I didn't realize what she was talking about until she told me to get her some stuff to take care of the crabs. I was eventually successful in procuring a remedy from another friend on the Kibbutz.

After finishing the Ulpan in six months, in 1974, I looked on a map for an interesting place to go. I found Nahal Yam, a small Moshav in the Sinai, south of El Arish on the Bardewill Peninsula, attached to the Mediterranean (there were about 5 Israelis & 5 volunteers there). I hitch hiked down, the first time, but it was in Occupied Egypt where there were many soldiers and I hitchhiked past an Israeli Patrol that saw me get into a car with 4 Arabs who picked me up & put me in the middle of the back seat. After 100 yards a taxi came screaming after us, cut us off, and told the driver that the soldiers wanted them to let me out immediately, which they did. I walked back & the patrol told me that it was very dangerous to accept rides from unknown Arabs. Many tourists had wound up dead in the desert, so they got me a ride with an Israeli jeep & I arrived at Nahal Yam in one piece! I stayed at the Moshav for about 6 months since my automatic return ticket to the States was fast approaching expiration. I decided to go back to Boston.

I remember, on New Year's Eve, that I bought a bottle of Johnny Walker Red Scotch and tried to encourage everyone to have a drink to celebrate "Sylvester" as they call it in Israel & Europe. However, no one else drank, so I got plastered on my own! The next day I had a hangover & stayed low, recovering. However, the 2nd day afterward, I went out on a fishing expedition, with the Israelis on our Moshav, in a special desert vehicle thru the desert to the ocean. I started to experience discombobulation of my senses.

I was smelling colors, tasting aromas, shaky on my feet & dehydrated, etc. It took me 2 more days to recover! The Israelis told me it was mentally, dangerous, to drink booze in the desert – that's why Islam forbids alcohol!

Another time we were out on a fishing boat and the net got caught. The Israelis were frightened to go under the water to fix it so I volunteered. I held my breath and it took me 2 attempts to swim down to the bottom, about 15-20 ft., where I untangled the net from some rocks. It was a scene out of Lloyd Bridges' old underwater diving shows on TV!

CAMBRIDGE 1974–75

I returned to the US & got an apartment with some friends on River Street in Cambridge near Central Square. I started driving for Boston Cab, nights. My buddy & roomie, Dave also drove for Boston Cab, but days, so I would come pick him up at 5 in the morning, then go back to the garage, where he would get his cab. I would turn mine in, then he'd drive me home, pick me up at 4 in the afternoon, & we'd do the same thing all over again! We had 2 other people living with us – a junkie, & a day tripper. At this time, an old friend of mine, Susie, moved in for a while!

Poem thyme: spicy,
electric or watt?
Susan Rosenberg/Jones,
no bones, no groans,
some moans from tones,
cornpones on loan -
phone home, Susan Jones!

There were also 4 young swingin' people who lived in the next apt. over where there were some wild, naked, trippin' parties between the 2 houses.

After a while I got very freaked out and lonely and started hearing voices so I went back to my parents' home where I was "getting signals from the TV" which scared the shit out me. At one point, I heard a voice tell me to pick up a knife & kill my father. I ran crying from the room. My parents took me to the VA Hospital where I was admitted immediately to the Psych. Ward where they asked me to put on PJ's & take a pill which I did; & then after I swallowed the pill, I asked what it was. They said "100 mg. of Thorazine", which freaked me out so I tried to run out of the ward! It took 12 people to restrain me. They threw me in a locked isolation room where I was literally trippin' - I was hallucinating on this Thorazine. I was allergic to it, I later found out.

Eventually, things quieted down a bit. A nurse & 2 aids would come to visit me several times a day for meals, etc. Once, when they were in talking to me & relaxed, I grabbed the keys out of the nurse's hand, pushed all three of them down, & ran out the door, closing it & locking them in. Then I calmly sauntered out of the ward, but I was caught before I got out of the hospital (like One Flew Over the Cukoo's Nest)

A few days later when I "improved", I went to my first Community Meeting, in the morning with all the doctors, nurses, staff & patients. So I was sitting in my bathrobe with nothing else on, when the Chief Resident said: "Good morning, Mr. T. How are you, today?" "Wonderful, I'm happy to be here – I believe in love, peace, & being open", then I stood up, my robe opened, & I streaked the whole meeting, running down the hall to my own room! After a month or so I was getting better but there were other sicko's in that place. A tough kid didn't like me & threatened to stomp me so I ran & hid under the bed of ole Irish, brogue – speakin' O'leary, who was sleeping. I felt an affinity for him for some reason & I hid under his bed for 2 hours until things quieted down.

Cliches are in the heir,
eyes in da mood, butt ware,
oh where, oh maiden fair, art thou verily
voracious, vociferous, yet ticklish?
Let loquacious licorice sweeten the pot.
Is not candy, dandy? Doodle away the hours,
where have all the flowers gone, but not forgotten.
Tell me watt, say what? I say, brother, can you
spare the time for all good people to party hearty, artsy, fartsy.
Don't be lazy, hazy, fazy, turn yur crazy into daisy!

JULIE'S SEDUCE

deduced by Toulous, albeit known knot two Zeus,
cooked Romeo's goose, whilst laced grapes turned to juice,
quite like Dean, Lenny Bruce.
Do you think me obtuse? or just a bit juiced?
perhaps I'z abstruse, my caboose needs a boost,
just like Bullwinkle Moose, till he fell from his roost–
silly rabbit is loose – he's Coo Coos, What 'bout you's?
What's da use? (no ewes, just sheepish grins from ear to hear)
Bee here now-all a-buzz & (ginsbergesque) howl!
Brown Cows on dee udder gut a hand it to yooz-barely dear,
we's, bear-ly deer, dare to wear corse hair of hare in Rabbit's
Lair -beware of veer of horse, where? Here, of course!

The Function of Unction

PILLROD Q. DOORLIP
TILLSOD J. FORETIP
MILLNOD L. SORESHIP
STILLPOD H. WHOREDIP
DILLBOD C. BORENIP
BILLCOD D. GOREWIP
ZILGROD Y. ROARHIP
YILPOD P. POORPIP
JILJAWED Z. YOURVIP
NILNAWED A. COREBLIP
WILLTOD P. NORYIP
GILROD E. TOREKIP
SHRILLSCROD W. SNORESLIP
KILLQUAD B. WARGRIP
SWILLFRAUD I. FLOORSTRIP
CRILLSHOD N. SCORETRIP
SKILLBROAD U. MOREHIP
STILL CRAWED after all dese years...

UMASS 1976

I returned to school at UMASS Amherst, taking psychology courses & working a job at the parking garage on campus where I listened to the UMASS radio station (WMUA). There, they played a lot of jazz, which I liked. So, I called the station to compliment them on their programming and got the General Mgr. He invited me to come down & hang at the station. I went over with an OZ of pot and ended up staying for 11 hours thru several shift changes & learning all about the equipment. Well I was hooked. It was a movement station, very politically left leaning. I liked that. Everybody smoked pot, & Jazz was coming out of every orifice! I ended up getting my own radio show, Jubilation in Jazz! I loved it.

I also got a part time job driving the Five College Bus where I was usually singing songs and being very friendly to all my passengers! One day a girl came up to me at the radio station and asked me if I was the bus driver who sang & would I give her a ride home to Northampton after the radio meeting? Sure! I found her attractive & I ended up getting into a hot & heavy relationship with Stacy. We loved to have sex in strange places like the car, in a tent, a corn field, the bedroom, the living room, a tent in the living room! But after a while, I left school to return to Israel!

On the same frigid wintry day in Europe, two different people, one in France and the other in England, both jumped into the water totally naked despite the elements and swam around till they were removed by the authorities. But only one of these people was turned over to the local mental health facility. Which one was committed and why? The Frenchman ...because he was in Seine!

ISRAEL 1977-78

I returned to Israel in '77 (with another Kitty Kat) to an Ulpan (class or studio) Gimmel (adv. level) at Kibbutz Ha-ogen, near Netanya. There I met my good friend, Naomi, another ulpanist volunteer. At first I tried to go out with her but she was just into being friends, so she became my kibbutz sister and we had kibbutz parents together, Bat-ami & Yair from Italy. They were some of the first settlers on the Kibbutz before 1948. It was neat.

I also met an older volunteer by the name of Tony E. who had lived in South Africa & was from England. He and I became friends & drinkin' buddies. After finishing the Ulpan I left for another Kibbutz, Menara, on the Lebanese border overlooking Kiryat Shmoneh. I became a volunteer/candidate for membership on the Kibbutz. I had Kitty Kat with me at this time, but she was pregnant. I took her up to visit the children's house, where I was a big brother to a 7 yr. old boy. Unfortunately a large dog attacked the Kitty before I could intervene, & I had to take the Kat outa there. She gave birth a few days later but none of the kittens lived.

I worked in the apple orchards which were right next to the Border Fence. In fact, a shed next to the fence had many bullet holes in it from previous attacks! I was not very happy on the Kibbutz. I had few friends & felt very isolated, so one day I took an overdose of some kinda pills. I slept for 3 days & nobody even looked to see if I was all right. I recovered but decided to leave the Kibbutz & go to Jerusalem.

I got a subsidized apt. on Lincoln Street opposite the YMCA soccer field in Rechavia, near the Old City. It was a great location & Kitty was with me again – hooray! First I got a job at Richie's NY Pizza, a Kosher joint where all the Americans & International kids hung out. There was a crazy bulletin board on the wall – it was a happenin place, but I only made $1 an hour. I learned to throw pizza dough in the air and get a good crust out of it! But a lot of wild street people came in and sometimes were quite aggressive. One time, a guy pulled the phone out of the wall cuz he was mad, & we ended up chasing him down the street until we finally caught him and held him for the authorities, but this was getting to me. I wasn't making enough for "hazardous duty pay", so I quit the pizza joint and got a job driving an international tour bus (cuz I had an International bus driver's license).

Well it was a French group who spoke no English or Hebrew except for the tour guide who spoke both English & Hebrew. I picked up the bus in the afternoon and took it back to my apt. cuz I had to leave at 3 AM in order to arrive up at Rosh Hanikra (the Club Med there), on time in the morning. Well I drove away from my apt., went around a bend, where there were railings next to the road, and I guess I scraped the side of the bus on the railings, but didn't realize it until the next day when I picked up my French group at Club Med & took them to Sfat in the Gallilee. After dropping the people off at a museum I drove around the corner to park but the streets are extremely narrow there and I went onto the sidewalk in making a turn. The cop on the beat had to move table & chairs out from the sidewalk cafe for me to get the bus by. Whew, I finally made it & parked the bus. Later I took the group to Kibbutz Ayelet Hashachar, where there was a guest house. On the way, the bus started smoking, and although I made it to the Kibbutz, they sent another bus & driver. I was fired cuz I didn't know how to fix the bus.

Then I got a job as a night desk clerk at the King's Hotel on Kikar HaTzarfat, around the corner from my apt. on Lincoln St. I worked from 10 PM till 7 AM, 6 nights a week. There were several Arab employees at the Hotel, some of whom I was friendly with, and saw them dating many guests at the Hotel, so when a Christian tour group of African Americans came thru, I befriended one middle aged woman, who later that night, called down to the desk where I was & requested that I bring her some tea. So I went up, got into an intense liplock &

hugging session for 10 minutes but I protested I had to get back to the front desk cuz the other guy at the desk, senior to me, already went over to the couch to take a nap, so I had to be at the front desk. Oh well!

I had some friends come to visit me from the Kibbutz for a few days where I had to sort of entertain them by day & work by night. By the time they left, I had not been getting much sleep (something which is very dangerous for me). I started getting very paranoid one night at the hotel. At 5 in the morning some German tourists had put in a wake-up call & I feared they were Nazis, out to get me. I made it thru till 7 am, had breakfast with the security guard, then went home, but I was so distraught that I thought I heard scraping noises from the street when I was trying to sleep. I thought it was a Nazi detail getting bodies.

I flipped out and my neighbor, an Argentinian woman teacher, took me to the Psychiatric Ward of a Hospital where I was admitted & had a rough time trusting the staff. I became aggressive, holding a group of patients in limbo, refusing to allow the staff to pass (because I was extremely paranoid) until they put me in 4 point restraints, very uncomfortable! I ended up spending 7 months in the Talbieh Psychiatric Hospital (a short walk from my apt in Jerusalem). I was strictly a vegetarian in the hospital for some mystical reason. I also played the piano there a lot.

So one day, I saw someone come in the locked door, and it didn't close immediately, so I pulled it open, & walked out to my apt. (just minutes away) where I found a note on the door from a young 18 year old girl I had met a few weeks before who wanted to visit me for a "massage". I was pissed that I missed her! So I went into my apt. & after a little while ended up lying on the bed not knowing what to do. Eventually, some one knocked at the door. It was a staff person from the hospital, urging me to return. I refused & they went away. But after several hours without my medication (I was on huge doses of psychiatric meds) I went back to the Hospital voluntarily & went back to the routine.

After 6 months or so, a visiting Psychiatrist from California asked if he could interview me & "present" me to the staff of the Hospital. I agreed & he recommended that I return to the US for further treatment. My parents arranged it & I went home to Boston soon thereafter. I spent 2 more months at the VA Hospital in JP. Then I came home & recovered!

Dark Ages: Knight Time

Is that seat saved? No, but we're praying for it!

Intermission: Walking throughthe gates of
San Juan Capistrano.

What Biblical character was fatherless?
Joshua who was the son of Nun!

Earning his major in music and minor in geology, the
youthful graduate looked for a job in a big
rock band.

The bridge playing musician, pondering whether to take
the trick or let it go, finally decided to trumpet.

For some singing groups, an encore is re-choired.
If you can't find anyone to sing with, you have to duet
yourself.

Berklee College of Music '79–'82

I returned to school at Berklee College of Music, majoring in piano. After one semester of practicing 6 hours a day and feeling like I wasn't even scratching the surface, I switched to audio recording with trombone as my main instrument. I got a work – study job on the stage crew of the Berklee Performance Center. It was great fun working with a lot of the big names in music like Dizzy Gillespie, Sonny Rollins, Smokey Robinson, B. B. King, Manhattan Transfer, et al. I took turns running a spotlite, helping out on security, sound & lites, being stage mgr (with the head phones), telling everyone when to start & stop. Once, Dizzy was warming up pianissimo, & incredibly fast, on the edge of the stage for me only, until I called the start of the show. Dizzy took one of the good looking female student crew members to LuLu Whites (a local Club) after the show.

*Billy
Taylor*

One time, when Sonny Rollins started to play, I was standing on the side of the stage playing along on air sax. I really cracked his wife up! At the time, I was living in a slum 2 room apt on Symphony road. A lot of the neighboring apts. were being gentrified but mine was holding out, cockroaches, mice, hookers & all! I became friendly with several hookers cuz they used to hang out on Hemenway/Boylston/Mass ave., the route I took to walk home from my work study job @ the Berklee Performance Center to my apt., 5 minutes away, after shows late at nite, often at 2 or 3 am. So I came upon a guy beating on a hooker one time. I pulled out my Swiss Army Knife and forced him to leave her alone. I told her to screw, she jumped in a cab while I commiserated with the dude about his getting ripped off by the hooker then he left & I went home. I never got rewarded for saving that hooker. Oh well, c'est la vie!

Harvey T.

QUIP TRIP

You can slip yur tip, whilst you sip yur nip,
just don't rip yur lip, while you dip yur hip,
cuz yur bip go Yippi-ki-yay go BOP!
To cop a buzz, be bop A-rooni,
au rooti, tutti-fruiti, already,
to bop a fuzz, re-boppin was scee bop a scuzz,
scidally scoo, shoo-bop a round,
humm fiddle-play-piddle!
poop, scat, shit, shat-pea disturbashun,
need EMANCIPATION!
Don't be fallen,
just bee pollen,
git ass haulin' - busy, ballin' the jack!

I also put people up for varying periods of time in my apt.
I put up an older woman veteran I met at the psych ward of the
VA Hosp. for several weeks helping her back on her feet. I also
put up a friend of mine – Jon R., who owned a moving truck,
for a while. Unfortunately he left my front door unlocked one
day & someone ripped me off for my new bass trombone worth
$1200, and my entire stereo hookup, including a turntable,
amp, receiver, speakers & reel to reel tape recorder – all worth
several thousand bucks! Jon eventually paid me a portion in
installments, but I was unable to replace most of the stuff.

I later joined the Symphony Tenant's Union & helped some
Hispanic people organize in other nearby urban locations.
Eventually I got depressed and alienated and dropped out of
school, moving back with my folks in1982, just before my Dad
died.

Take time to pause from yur daily chaws tis a sound idea, cuz
society's flaws, like cat's paws & sharks jaws, buzzards' laws,
cruel guffaws, create shores of Shah's with sharp cutting saws.
Must need heed artist's draws, attempts at gauze.
Maw 'n Paw in the land of Oz, as the Raven caws ...Nevermore!

5:55 PM 22 May 82 tri-node dirge: ode to Dadio'(d)

MO' boned base line mode
doncha know dat he showed our load/OUI owed/ gnu, knowed?
or no'd. Twould forbode seeds sowed, green growed, Poah Toad,
Woe whowed...

ABBA PAPA dada POP–
Moshe Kosher, keemat flop,
da-di dadio so stop.
PATER FRATER MATER HOP!
Ma & Pa, what a kettle o' fish, we've got me into!

Gone Fishin'

Da bluz, a constant, sigh, at ease,
can't stand dat, dem, dere, doze, & deze,
dat clap thy thighs (trez tight)don't bite,
just flight agin' & again,
dee press she on da way of Zen–
gives rise to itch,
to yearn 'n learn 'n feel a yen for...
horsemen do knot an apocalypse make
butt ciggies 'n druggies, dey seal da fate of
Nuclear ventri-ficular

GONE FISSION!

Mit ein tochis-auf zwanzig yorenzik!
Your rear end can only be on one road at a time!

–old Yiddish Proverb, quoted by Richard A. Cohen
aka Whitey Bulger, aka Steve Slyne

Coffine & Nicitacco have recently been associates
of Charley the Tuna (CHAS -Q- LUNA) who,
according to Al Sleet, the hippi-dippi whether(oar knot) man,
has recently been swimming in a sea of madness,
in the state of confusion, contusion, illusion!
Craziness is compassionate
for all the normality that must be endured
until loving presence can be opened on X-mas (que nada)!
Down with gravity! Up wit levity! So where's da brevity?

What's yur beef?

---

*Hey, didja hear the one about the guy who wanted to
stop eating poultry? He chickened out, & quit cold
turkey. (foul humor)*

BRAIN DRAIN REFRAIN FROM SANE

The family dat smokes together,
chokes together!
smokin' & chokin', tokin' 'n jokin',
Are the folk in? Are you fukin' or pukin'?
Far Friggin' out a cite!
Phrygian bout o' slight fragmentary plight.
Spank ewe very mucho Groucho, ouch-
oh hell-in tents passed sense of humor.

Before that time I smoked cigarettes, had asthma, and quite frequently had breathing attacks sending me into the Emergency Room of the JP VA Hospital for a .3 shot of Epinephrine, a coupla hours of intravenous amminophyllin, & then I was good as new. On the way out of the hospital I used to bum a smoke, HoHo! I finally quit smoking cigarettes when I was spending time on the psych. ward and stayed up all nite with a member of AA who inspired me to quit cold turkey after many unsuccessful attempts. I finally succeeded! Hooray!

I also answered an ad for a jazz DJ in 1979 at WMFO, Medford (the Tufts University student radio station) and became a regular there for 12 years. I had several shows, including – Just Jazz, Jubilation in Jazz, Radio Free Jazz, Jazz Variations. "On the Town" was a live local band show, and I did fill-ins for Morning After Blues & Freeform Radio.

I also did much production of PSAs (public service announcements) many – movement related promos – eg, the June 12th Campaign against Nukes at the UN special session on disarmament, demonstration against Gov. King's workfare war against the poor, US out of El Salvador, etc. In addition, I was the production mgr. & technical teacher for new students. It was quite loose at that movement station. We would as likely be giving someone a massage as smoking a joint or doing wild & crazy radio. One time I came to the station late at night & started adding graffiti all over the walls, ceilings, bathrooms, offices. Every room at the station had something about SPAM! I spammed the entire station! Later that week spam graffiti started appearing on the record jackets & every other conceivable place you could think of, it was a SPAM Revolution: I've got the whole world in my SPAM, How SPAM can you get? I can't give you anything but SPAM, You ain't nuthin' but a SPAM dog! All you need is SPAM! & da SPAM me Blus!

Shalom & welcome to HBT's swingin' rock & roll dance party. I'm Harvey T., your friendly, neighborhood, jazz, bluz, & Klezmer, DJ Rabbit spinnin' the oldies for y'all; so put on your dancin' shoes & lets kick up a ruckus ! Hit it, Jack! Here's lookin' at ya, with some inspiration to get you gyratin & perspicatin', so enjoy the ploy, oy, boy!

We were playing baseball. A fly ball hit a flock of ducks in mid-air, killed one, and injured two others. The umpire promptly ruled that the hit was a fowl ball.

– Undertakers usually have a grave attitude even if they are dying to get your business.

During this time I drove a school bus for Arnold Transportation in Dorchester. One of the other drivers, a big, fat black man, by the name of Jelly Belly, was a blues singer on the side.

I was very decompensated from being at Berklee and my Dad's passing. I went to a day treatment program at the VA & Lincoln St. outpatient clinic downtown & at Court St. & was psychiatrically disabled at this time. I got put on Social Security Disability Insurance & was in intensive therapy, individual & group for several years.

Out of my mind. Back in five minutes.

All generalizations are false.

I'm as confused as a baby in a topless bar.

I don't suffer from insanity, I enjoy every minute of it.

If ignorance is bliss, why aren't more people happy?

BU CPR R&T Program 1985–87

I finally entered the Occupational Rehabilitation program at BU called the R&T (Research & Training) program where I met Larry & Dori & Karen Danley & Anne & Kim & the Director, Dr. Bill. All of the staff were great and they really helped me a lot. I used to enter the class and stand around until everyone else sat down cuz I couldn't decide where to sit (as if it were of extreme importance)! Eventually I lost this hangup, became less inhibited, & sat down in any chair. I had made progress!

Later I went back to UMASS Amherst but had problems with my roommates at Swiss Village. I had another nervous breakdown and had to go into the Northampton VA hospital for a few weeks. Then I left school again & went home. Larry & Anne from BU drove up from Boston to Northampton to help me get out of the hospital & give me a ride back home to Boston. I'll be eternally grateful for that! I went back to the program now called the Continuing Education Program (CEP) of the Center for Psychiatric Rehabilitation (CPR) of Boston University, where they helped me get skills together & gave me a job as an interviewer for a while. I returned to UMASS Boston, finishing up my last 4 courses for a BA in Psychology in 1988. But I was still a little shaky emotionally cuz when I was taking the methods lab course I needed to use the computers, I was extremely paranoid of them & upon several occasions went to sit at the computer & got scared off cuz they didn't respond properly!

DAY OF EVACUATION OF BUNKER HILL TO THE CASTLE

Dressed to da gills, pop full with pills,
Historical Morals presented by Drs. Art & Bill,
The eulogies were read, about the dresses – 'nuff said!
All 'ceptin' few got diplomas to mill,
And so all I can say is prepare to FULFILL!

USPS-Millis-1989-90

My old family dentist, Dr. Shea, is a real hot ticket. He's always been interested in me, & when I told him that I applied for a job as a rural route carrier with the Post Office, he suggested I talk to the Postmaster with a real go-getter attitude. "I'm your man", Dr. Shea told me to tell the Postmaster, so I did, & would you believe it, after initially being a little negative with me, the Postmaster gave me the job! I'm sure it was my enthusiastic presentation, urged on by Dr. Shea, that got me that job! My shrink certified that I was recovered enough to work a full time job such as that with USPS. I lasted almost 2 years until I saw my medication, Prozac, on the front cover of Newsweek. I freaked out, froze at my desk & was catatonic, not responding to anyone. They called an Ambulance, which took me from Millis to Boston's Faulkner Hospital where my shrink met me and gave me a tranquilizer which calmed me down. However, from that point on I began missing work, occasionally, due to anxiety attacks, so they tried to fire me. I applied for a Disability Annuity (Pension) and was awarded a small pension as long as I didn't return to work at full pay, but I could work part time. While I was working at the Post Office, I joined the Weight Loss Clinic & lost 43 lbs. in 4 months! Unfortunately, I put it all back, plus more, in a year. When I lost all the weight, I went to my sister's 3rd wedding in LA in 1989 to Joe S.

At this time I was very active at my Temple, Hillel B'nai Torah (HBT). The Cantor/ Shammas, Haskel, (a holocaust survivor & a Lamed Vavnik, one of the hidden 36 saints upon whom the grace of the world depends) used to call me to come help make a quorum of 10 men for the twice daily Minyan. I was a mainstay of the Minyan, along with several old timers, elderly men going everyday, in the morn. & evening, until we became liberated, went egalitarian, & began counting women!

Haskel A. (z'''l)'s birthday was Dec. 24, 1924. He was born in Lodz, Poland and was the Cantor, Shammas, & Minyan Maven for Temple Hillel Bnai Torah for 25 years until 1995 when he retired. Then he read Torah & Megilla for Temple Emeth, until his death on the 2nd day of Shavuot, 7 Sivan, 5762 (May 17, 2002 @10:30 PM, a Friday nite)

Haskel was a Holocaust Survivor and came to the US in 1953. He married Betty in 1955. They had 2 sons, Alan, who died young of a tragic illness, & Mark, a Yiddish Theater Director in New York! Haskel liked classical & klezmer music & knaidlach from the Butcherie. Haskel read Torah as smoothly as you may eat cheesecake or chicken soup with matzah balls, pullet & kreplach, flunken with tzimmes, gefillte fish & herring, whitefish, pike & carp, lokshun kugel, knishes, corned beef, brisket & stuffed cabbage, kasha varnishkas, pumpishkas, galoshes, gosh, its all gettin' me hungry! We'll miss you, Haskel!

The president of the Shul appointed me to the Board of Directors & I became friendly with Toby who urged me to co-produce a fund raising concert at the Temple with 2 Klezmer Bands – The Klezmer Conservatory Band & Shirim Klezmer Orchestra, two of the best Klezmer bands in the country, based in Boston. I got both bands to appear separately, & together for the last number. It was the first time these two bands played together & everyone was excited about the KLEZFEST! It was a huge success, we sold 250 tickets, had a program book, and made over $3000. I was to go on to produce more Klezfests for the next 7 years.

During this time I got a part time job at the Instructional Resource Center (IRC), part of BU's Sargent College of Allied Health Professions. My boss was Lucia G., a great photographer who ran the darkroom & IRC. I became a media specialist utilizing the slide projectors, VCR 's & video editing suite & assisting in the Library. Another woman that worked there was very attractive but a real bitch & after 2 years I became so unhappy that I resigned because I couldn't get along with her. I was also working part time (6 hr./week) at the Synagogue Council of Massachusetts in the office, but was fired due to poor attendance. Again, I had anxiety attacks & couldn't help it. So by 1993 I was totally unemployed again, and still disabled.

In 1995, I got a letter from Social Security asking if I had worked in the past 5 years. Well my little part time jobs didn't seem necessary to report at the time but after I informed Soc. Sec about my 2 part time jobs they claimed I had worked over the limit & therefore I had been overpaid some $33,000. I was so taken aback & upset that I tried to commit suicide. I drank a bottle of wine with an OD of pills. My mom found me crumpled up on the floor of the basement, unconscious, so she called the police, who took me to the hospital. I recovered relatively slowly.

For the next few years I didn't work, except for an occasional band gig. I played the trombone in a band, Klozet Klezmer that donated the proceeds to Charity. I also took a free TV/Video Production course at Newton Cable Access TV & worked on a short documentary with my cohort – Mark M., about saving Hancock Woods, a 27 acre tract of wetland being considered for development in 1996. The neighborhood group that fought the developers won the battle & the land was taken over by the State/Feds as protected wetlands.

The wailing wall of sound, LSJCC fig newton B.Y.O. (Prunes) X eclectic, phrenetic, energetic, diaretic, Klezmeropolis, banned on top of old Smokey. It fell off the Shmelkee & onto the Fleur de Lise…is a good name fer da hall of fame band. Klozet Klez doesn't close quite correctly in close quarters, kind a classy Klezmer-Shirim sure sounds sassy, some skewed smooth jazz y KCB initialed an eventual evaluation eliciting electronic and superimposed sonic BOOM, BANG, BOP-Reskop da top don't stop, just shop RE-BOP a diddli, DO BOP SHOO BAM, Grand Slam basin' a ball on watt a kosher ham IAMBIC PENTAMETER is! Just define parameter! 'tis the Klezmerantic, Klezmerific, Quintessential, Quintet.

I later joined a band of Mental Health Consumers in Cambridge called Tunefoolery! I played occasional gigs on the trombone and later did a Klezmer duo with me on the keyboard & the Director of Tunefoolery (a staff person named Theresa) on violin. We played gigs at mental health centers, nursing homes, hospitals, social service agencies, schools & conferences; & we got a small stipend for each gig, money raised from corporate sponsors!

....

Yaz says – JAZZ has pazazz wit razzamataz!

Herb Herd that dere's a Mingus among us whereas a hunk of Monk-y funk makes Miles smiles whilst Trane wails off about Bird flying to the Max waxing sentimental. Is he Dizzy? Match the catch w/Satch-Mo bones-smokin', tokin' like a broken record. Prez says Le'z be friends. Count Duke out-a-site, while Brubeck takes five!

My obstetrician moonlights as a stand-up comic, his jokes are not very funny, but I love his delivery
… (Aardvark: Strenuous labor).

MONK-y FUNK

A hunk of funky Monk, no bunk! (unlike monkey funk),
trickles down, tickling sound, trinkling, tinkling, frequently
found, funiculi funicularum, straight no chaser in the bar
room, (car tomb blew fume, Kartoom cartoon), a buffoon
may loom, sew soon oui stretch dee fabric of cocoon,
Chinese chow foon at noon, a boon to be dee C jam blus
(or R doze Basie bagel cues?) perchance, strawberry, jelly,
belly clues, signs of jelly roll Mingus, hues of Sphere, air
apparent here, ethereal in the roundness, effervescence in
the soundness-refuse boo's, don't snooze or lose nor
abuse...whose dues? You's formerly Zeus with shoes who
slew dee dragon on and on and yawn, rather than note a
natural, sharply, flattened quote abounding Thelonius
brilliance, Brilliant Corners, resounding resilience!

Here's what's salient to the spherical valiant: shall we stall
Silly ants on call while, we fall father & further away from
stallions on valiums (mare's bare hair)

Nutty iz relatively Functional!
get cha Charley Parker yarmulkes, here!
get cha Abdullah Ibrahim caftans, there!
get cha John Coltrane beanies, everywhere!

Sects, sects, sects – Is that all you monks ever think about?

Have you heard about the new computer TV that fixes
itself? It's a Christian Science monitor.

Finally I took over the Shammas job at the Temple & continued being active as a volunteer, helping to produce, do sound & play in the Klezmerific Quintet for another fundraising concert series produced by George C. (called a nite of eclectic music, with 3 different bands). Also during this time, I was a member of a marching band that did 25 parades a year. Tony, our 82 yr. old bandleader, is a real character, dressing in drag for the Unity parade in Cambridge, when the South Boston Saint Patty's day parade refused to allow Gay & Lesbian marchers. If there's any free food anywhere to be had, Tony always finds it! We always ate well...

Fat chance I'll join Weight Watchers!

My niece Rachel has a 5 year old boy, Jake, 2 twin, 3 year old girls, Maddy & Becca; and just had another baby girl, Olivia Grace Aug.11, '02. My brother is their grandfather & he has two other daughters, Karen, & Adrienne (who got married last year & adopted a bulldog puppy, named Ginger)!

here's a poem:

Dick towers over his grand dog, Ginger-ly gyratingly gravitating towards genteel, gentle, green giants who horn in on da corn, as dey stalk ocha-chornya poets, baseball balks, alcoholistic box of rain, same train of thought refrain from inane brain in pain on plane wit insane chrain from Spain. Is Cain mainly able, two bits into honey whether Groucho makes marks in vain, or knot two try bow tie (TYBO?) THAI Bo-peep! bulldog, sheep in wolverine creep. Keep on truckin'! Steep tea. Bow wow & how, now, brown cows on dee udder hand, tickle guppies & puppies of yuppies! yippi's fer hippies! bippi's fer bop-sters, tipsy atop, stir it up, sir!

You can do the dew,
and can hoosker do.
You can shoo-bee-doo,
and can Frodo, WHO?
you can wail boo hoo,
though I kinda doubt,
tune yer piano, too...but
cha just can't tuna fish! – POP!

What is the definition of a Jewish jersey? It is the woolen garment worn by a child when its mother is cold.

You have the right to remain silent. Anything you say will be misquoted, then used against you.

"I won't let a flat tire get me down," Tom said, "without despair!"

Feinstein was crossing Collins Avenue in Miami Beach and was struck by a passing auto. Several passersby came to his rescue and laid him down on a bus bench. A kindly silver-haired matron approached the injured man and asked, "Are you comfortable?" "Eh!" sighed Feinstein, "I make a living."

On a mat I pee, a literary agent, you see.
A sneeze, da Truth – it be so cruel,
I feel a wee bit burnt, & bummed, & spurned –
The sum of all, a tool, a fool, a feeble fawn –
I fall but 'ow pray tell will end? 'tz-all!

Stories about me & the Ma- a Jewish Mother and a frustrated son, oy veh!

My Mom is a "gutah neshamah" (a good soul). She has helped me out countless times when I was ill or had problems. She came to visit me, bringing food every day, when I was hospitalized at the Veteran's Hospital in Boston on several occasions for months at a time!

She was born in Montreal, Canada where her parents moved after eloping from Russia to London, England. My grandfather (Reuven Ben Zion) deserted from the Russian army to elope with my grandmother Rachel. They had several children: Maurice, Louis (who was killed in a car crash when he was only in his 20's), Jennie (my Mom), Abraham (Sam), David, & Ethel. Maurice married Edith & settled in Denver having 2 kids, Leslie & Debby. Debby married Steve & had a daughter, Marne! Uncle Sam married Bea & had Linda. Uncle Dave married Mollie & had 4 daughters: Fay, Bevy & Lynn (all nurses), & Toby, an

Grandma and cousin Leslie

elementary school teacher. Lynn is married to Norm & has 2 kids, Jennie & Kim. Lynn is also interested in Genealogy & has extensive records on the whole family! Toby is married to Joe & also has 2 kids, David & Samantha! Ethel was married to Uncle Ben & had 2 kids, Jeff & Dennis, (who married Karen & Susan) had 2 kids each, Robert, Danielle; David & Rachel! Dennis remarried & adopted 2 other kids. Jeff's son, Robert married Dana & they just had a baby boy, Benjamin Walter!

My Mom is the only one left alive of her siblings. They moved from Montreal to Boston, then Laconia, N.H. where my Mom grew up – attending Laconia High School & Plymouth Normal School (now Plymouth State Teacher's College). She met her 1st husband (Ben L.) after working as an elementary school teacher in a single room school with 26 kids, all in different grades & all sitting in the same room! My Mom had 2

Mom and dad

kids before me, Roberta & Richard. Roberta had 2 kids, Randi
& Barry; & Dick married Jude, having 3 kids: Rachel, Karin &
Adrienne (married to Devin & they just had a new baby boy,
Tyler Louis, born 9 June 03 @ 3:01AM–8lb., 7oz.) Rachel
married Dan & they have 4 kids: Jacob, Rebecca, Madeline,
and Olivia.

Ben L. was a drummer & projectionist, but he was ill with
complete leakage of the heart valves, & unfortunately he passed
away in the early 40's. My mom was a single parent with 2
small children for several years until she met my dad, Morris P.
He was a meat cutter from Russia who came to this country as
a teenager! He opened a meat store in Allston called the Legion
Market – values in meat that can't be beat – where I worked as
a 10 & 11 yr. old & was proud as punch to "wait on trade",
until the place burned down in 1961. The night before the store
burned, I was cleaning up, swept the floor, & dumped the
ashtray in the wastebasket. I was petrified after I heard that the
store burned down. I thought I was somehow responsible becuz
of that ashtray that I emptied in the trash, but years later I found
out that the fire department had determined that the fire started
in the walls from faulty wiring! Whew!

My dad didn't have much education but he was a loyal,
conscientious, hard working, family man. He was the youngest
of 5 kids all born to Eshea & Sarah in Novogrudik, White
Russia. Dad's siblings included Minnie who married Israel, the
photographer; Ethel, who married Sam, the Communist; Joe
who was the first in the family to move to the US living in
Beverly, MA & having 1 daughter; and Rose who married
Maurice – they had 3 kids, Ernie, Jack, & Sylvia who had 3
kids, each – Department of redundancy, department! Now
there are grandchildren all around!

After his meat market burned down, Dad went to work for
my Uncle Ben who owned a small chain of 13 supermarkets
called the Capital Markets! Uncle Ben employed practically his
whole family and several other families as well! At different
times my mom, dad, brother, sister, & myself all worked for my

uncle, either at the Capital Supermarkets, office or warehouse. Unfortunately my uncle got sick, & the business went bankrupt – c'est la vie!

My dad passed away in 1982, right after I dropped out of Berklee College of Music, & and I moved back in with my Mom. I was mentally ill again in 1984 (Orwellian Shudder!). I went thru many years of "Psychiatric Disability" until I stabilized somewhat in the mid 90's. I started doin' more around the house until eventually I was running the household.

Around 1999 my Mom slowed down & stopped driving. She gave my niece, Karin, her "86 Toyota with less than 45,000 miles the next year, & "Gramma" Jean started gettin' shaky on her legs, requiring a walker in the house, & wheelchair out of the house, but she was very sharp and had all her faculties, although she tended to be a bit depressed about her advanced age & continuing physical deterioration. She occasionally had a memory lapse, everyone does at times, & she berated herself for "losing my mind", but I assured her she was sharp as a tack & she never let me get away with anything.

It was a bit frustrating at times when I was downstairs on the phone & she would pick up the receiver to tell me she needed me only to say (when I went up to see what was the matter) Do the laundry, the dishes, the shopping or some other such non urgent matter. Or I was downstairs for a few minutes relaxing and she would ring the bell I gave her for emergencies. What was the problem? *'Please close the shades & open the windows or clean up in the kitchen'* – fastidious, she was a kvetch at times, and I was a schlumpah, oy what a mess! But I love her very much. She took care of me all my life when I was in many rough situations. She stood by me, so I want to stand by her! But, brother do I need patience!

Poem fer MaMa:

mummy i cry, please be well!
mummy i cry, who can i tell?
mummy i cry, who will kvell
from nachas from children from...
I should know...sigh, at ease
will ya pleas eat your goober peas-
donchu knock those knees,
just let grow the trees
of knowledge and peace!

mimicry, should i try?
mimicry, would i lie?
mimicry, don't wanna die
but living ain't easy-
oft makes me queasy, so much is sleazy, sigh,
bees travel at G's to make honey, but not fer us diabetix.
I guess it all comes down to genetics.
MaMa, mi mummy, emah sheli,
Mother is such a dear word,
so I've heard...I should know, go with the flow,
but when the wind blows...not always so HO HO HO-
More like whoa, slow, and even NO! time to go...

Listening to Nat King Cole and the Bluz O'mighty from
Oliver Nelson's More Bluz and the Abstract Truth on new
tears eve with Ma-Ma, GLOBAL TV NETWORK LINKUPS-
know news is good news,
The year 2000 in the Julian Calendar
is the year 5760 in the Jewish Calendar.
When did the world begin according to Garp?
Quit harpin' on that Karp fella,
sounds a bit fishy if'n youse ask me.
I wood if I cod, do it for the halibut!

Time fer da suicidal bluz, doze institutional, sexist, racist, authoritarian, & thoroughly demoralizin' dues dat one must eschew or iz dat choose to lose da booz is news butt cues from Jews in pews who snooze, dey lose a fuse to blues O'Mighty!

Passin'over the holiday

Twas the night after Seder, and all through the house
Nothing would fit me, not even a blouse.
The matzah, the farfel, the charoset I ate,
after both the Seudarim, had gone to my waist.
When I got on the scales, there arose such a number!
When I walked over to shul (less a walk than a lumber),
I remembered the marvelous meals I'd prepared;
the turkey with gravy, the beef nicely rared,
The wine and the matzo balls, the Migdal pareve cheese,
The way I'd never said, "I've had enough; no more, if you please."
I tied on my apron again, & spied my reflection disgustedly, then,
I said to myself, "You're such a weak wimp,"
"You can't show up at shul resembling a blimp!"

So, away with the last of the meatballs so sweet,
Get rid of the turkey, chopped liver and meat.
Till all the additional ounces have vanished.
I won't have any more macaroons from the box,
I can't wait till next week. (Ah, the bagels and lox.)
I won't have any luchsen, farfel or p'chach,
I'll munch on a carrot or wire shut my own jaw.
I've got no time to kill if I want to diet
If I have to cook one more chicken, I think I will riot.

PERSONAL ADS (1990-2002)

WALKING PARTNER + for tall, spontaneous, SJM, 40 (39)/41 read sjm, formerly 40, looks 39 and feels 41; musician, social scientist, volunteers of America, JCC Special Needs, VISTA, performance technician, student of rational (papr-eek-a), positive interpersonal, interactional, humanistic, martian growth offshoots of KLEZ-JAZZ: NIGGUN FER A REPRESSED PERSONHOOD.

When Kermit, the green, met Eric, the red,
in the service of Robin da hood,
twas Yogi, the bare on Blueberry hill,
slippin' Goofy, the grape, a good bill
from Donald, the duck, no luck when Buddy, the rich,
caught Porky, the pig, slippin Minnie, the mouse,
a mickey from Peter, the pan, a fan of Man of La Munch
a bunch of lunch. Wood Pinnochio hammer out an
arrangement for Victoria to principally score with Snow
White & the seven dwarves? Only Elke, the chemist knew
fer sure the lore of the former whore, Fannie the flag, a hag
who brags & nags with drags on bags dat lags and zigs not
zags, no sags, nor rags too riches!

Tall, spontaneous SJM, 49 seeks SJF over 39, who likes bluz, jazz & Klezmer music & is progressive, sensual, and compassionate. A BIG PLUS if you can walk the blues on any instrument including voice!

6'2" tall, SJM, 50 -left leaning, affectionate & kind, loves music, is seeking a Woman for terms of endearment!

Walking partner & good kisser sought by tall, SJM 51, progressive, compassionate & spontaneous – into Jazz, Bluz & Klezmer

66

There's nuthin' plain about Jane!
I'll bet yer waitin' fer another refrain.
We could turn it into Bluz & talk about a train,
or fly it thru the skies & label it a plane,
but to me, let's call it the play'n!
and here's yet another restrained refrain!
The rain in Spain stays mainly on the brain,
no pain, in vain, no strain, no drain.
What do ya think? Insane? No just inane! that's Jane!

Attentive Lover, SJM, 51, 6'2", left-leaning, jazz/blues
afficianato, seeks compatible woman for loving relationship!

If Music be the food of love, play on...tall SJM, 51, left-leaning,
seeks loving woman for terms of endearment

A fine is a tax for doing wrong.
A tax is a fine for doing well.

I started out with nothing, and I still have most of it.

It was recently discovered that
research causes cancer in rats.

Sigh-mon & Garfunkle (or Izzy a Carbunkle?) Donut play
punk for funk-y Monk-y skunk. Shekels fer piece o' da pie.
Peace in da sky, pleas from on high, please not to cry!
better to sigh, than to die. Elvis, oh my!
Pelvis, she lies with da size of her ayes. Bountiful Blighs,
mutinous thighs, dim-wit Catchin' Rye's, pliant porpoise on
purpose.

Courses on Chirpas
jokin' wit Burp's:

Bring it up agin & we'll vote on it!
6 more & we'll have 7-up!
Up, Up, & Away.
squeeze me, scuzemous? Parley Tu?
Burp-eh-vous!
If you was down dere, you'd wanna come up, too!
The rest will be up latah, gatah!
Burpee's seedin' the hare's lair.
out of da mouth of Babes...
Cha get any on ya?
Hope everything came out OK!

Do ewe care if oui tear a pair of hair from da rear of barely dear, here we fairly dare to gear our merely Seer of Lublin/ Naphtule's dreamin' of Brandwein accordingly: May Reb Nachman of Bratslav & the Baal Shem Tov be a blessing for World Peace (Let Green Peace be a motzie fer whirled peas)

Tall, spontaneous SJM, 51, left-leaning, affectionate, & kind, music- lover, is seeking a woman for terms of endearment.

Smoking Partner & Good Kisser sought by tall, ns, 51 yr. old SJM, progressive, affectionate, & electrifyingly musical, watt iz hip?
HIP is JAZZ & BLUES in poetic shoes

Searching for the perfect kisser, tall, SJM, 51, spontaneous, progressive, & affectionate, loves jazz, bluz & Klezmer, seeks significant other.

Nurd's absurd bird turd or is dat heard word?
Curd served from Harvey's Tea rabid Rabbit droppings, windy
wit, a breazy bit sopping up the hit 40 animals on Noah's ark
in da park. Hark, the bark of a shark in da dark on a lark, its a
stark quark! Girdles purport to freely forensicate, while
attorneys at law, refute plastic, spastic, elastic, bombastico
burritto, acidic ate, to & thru a few blue Sioux in lieu of
Hugh. Sue knew a boo fearing crew who raised a hue, den
cried Wolfman Jack! Moo on dee udder hand, no bull, cows
da wolf, she say howl, & dee owl? He say Who?

Mista Ogden knashed his teat,
he knew he wood a knot tie his feat,
And so instead, he tried to beat da heat,
& what did he get, for all this sheet?
Insipidity, pure disturbated moot foot, toot poot, Kant refute,
what a beaut, ewe kid, surely you jest!
Ewe suck sheep, close to the chest! 'tis da best!

Ware was Caesar's salad at the thyme
was it sage to assuage the page, peppered with saucy retorts.
Red whine in any port, white brine of any sort,
scallions mine, Rosemary's short, baby!

Jews on da juice, choose to be loose
when it comes to abstruse goose abuse
for an obtuse moose on caboose
with a deuce, tis no use, nor a ruse, just da blues!

Which is verse, witch is worse
bitch, perverse, hitch a nurse,
twitch a horse, rich divorce.
May the force bee wit you,
sweet as a honey lamb, (funny-ewe don't look sheepish!)

Mosquitos suck, Miles smiles, Trane wails off
whilst dere's a Mingus among us,
cucumbers humongous, encumbers the fungus
dat flung us our tongues!

THYME FER A POEM

Spicy or watt? Electric & herbal! There's a MINGUS,
among us, cunning-lingus humongous.
Do you think cukumbers suck juice?
Lettuce is ahead in the race. Tochis in arrears, it appears dat
dere's bears barely here, sadly tears at my hairs that're oh so
barely there, do I dare to use nair on my hare, where Harvey T.
Rabbit wears fairware haircare, here, there & dear (deer horn
in on antlers while the rooster usta be bullish, now he's
sheepishly horsin around da pigpen-playin cat 'n dog with pet
peeves)!

Nevermore dee Edgar Allen Poe House, not to be confused
with the County House for the Indigent or the local House of
Ill Repute, Po' House or 'Ho House, so douse da louse on
mouse wit souse & drink da blinkin' stinkin', sinkin, freakin,
Peek-a-boo! in lieu U can sue, who? Ewe, a sheepish grin will
win ya lots of hot spots, wasted spaced shots not tots, not
lying about cots, knot tying the rope of hope that helps to
cope wit dope'n such as much-PO' HOUSE BLUZ! Its not
about making cents, dollars to ponies 'n phonies-auntie up,
relatively pecuniary in nature, makes me bleary eyed inside,
so oui sighed, must abide...re-tried beens every pun.
(Flying Burritto Brothers' beans, anyone?)!

NOBLE GOO

No Bull goo, butt cows on dee udder hand squeeze milk from a stoned, herbal brew (Ha Ha) with just a few drops of dew (La La), from a true blue hue of you who knew da crew from da zoo, Yogi, can ewe bear Boo Boo too? You know who, Nu? Tochis by the Coo-cue Koo-Koo) A stool-pigeon was sitting at a bar, talking to the wall, when a barfly flew in, flamboyantly flaunting French flambois for flaccid florists on fridays, frequently frustrating Fred Flintstone's foibles, quite flaggellently!

> Attentive Lover: Tall, SJM, 52, progressive, left-leaning, affectionate & kind, loves jazz & blues, seeks good kisser for LTR.

Brenda Harlow Infatuation Situation

I like your eyes, your thighs, your size, your sighs, your why's, you're wise – Wherefore art thou, oh wow! The possibilities, the silly sensibilities, The bluz ain't nuttin' but a refrain train payin' dues on the Coltrane brain, jazz-me blus,
blue suede shoes, I love you's, scoobee doo's to you too, Boo Boo's...by dat silly Sackbutt, Rabbit, Harvey T.

> Attention healthy women over 40: relieve the pressure of Menopause: (Let me lick your troubles away).

> Progressive, tall, SJM, 52, attentive lover, seeks good kisser for a LTR.

> Do infants enjoy infancy as much as adults enjoy adultery?

> If love is blind, why is lingerie so popular?

Andrea (Kenberma, 67 & Providence 71). I met Andrea down Nantasket Beach. She was my friend, Ronny 's girlfriend for a while. I went out with her, wrote her many letters & she wrote me many in return while I was in the Marines & particularly in Vietnam. So when I came back to the States after getting out of the Marine Corps I made a date to visit her at her family's home in Providence. Her parents & sister were very gracious & she took me to see Love Story, after which I asked her to marry me, but she was flabbergasted and couldn't respond other than a lame "I don't know". So we drifted apart after that and I later found out she married a veteran.

> **"I am"** is reportedly the shortest sentence in the English language. Could it be that "I do" is the longest sentence?

Stacy (UMASS AMHERST-1976-77) met me at WMUA, Amherst while she was living in Northampton & I was driving a 5 college Bus & working as a DJ at the UMASS radio station. She followed me to Israel a year later after I dropped out of school & emigrated to Israel supposedly, but when she came to visit, I started having emotional problems which drove her away forever! One of my regrets is that I didn't marry her!

We made love in a car, in a jar, from afar, rite on par, at a bar, hardly marring the tarmac! Oh! her face! not a trace, of a space, in a vase, in case you're right on base/tight embrace! Oh the Chase!

Ogden Knashed his teat, beat his best behest, neat, his nest abreast/feat instead of dressed like a pest in a vest on the chest of the fressed who have missed the test. Meet the rest, Shirley, ewe jest about the guest riding the crest of the zest in the west!

Tilly (Singer 1990-91). I met Tilly in a Klezmer Ensemble, she was the singer (in Yiddish) & I was the trombone player. We had a gig one time & met in Brookline; she needed a ride home, which I gave her, then I called her to go out to a movie and on returning to her house after the flick, we smoked a number & started massaging each other. It was hot & steamy sex from then on until she started getting on top & pinning me. I was claustrophobic & ended our relationship immediately. Unfortunately I didn't communicate properly. I really wish I had worked it out with her, but c'est la vie!

If a pig loses its voice, is it disgruntled?

My baker dozen give me thirteen anymore!

Shotgun wedding: A case of wife or death.

What is a computer virus? A terminal illness.

A pessimist's blood type is always B-negative.

Sea captains don't like crew cuts.

Gwen (from da bakery, 2001) I was totally infatuated with a young girl that worked in a nearby bakery. I brought her flowers one day & she seemed very appreciatively friendly, so I wrote her a poem & gave her my resume & asked her out for dinner, but she told me she was engaged. I was crushed. I didn't go into that bakery again for over a year. Man, was she beautiful -Let's rite a poem about Gwen, a friendly flower who brightens my day with her warm personality and contagious smile!

When Gwen, no hen, met Ben, my friend, ten men, then Zen transcend my yen fer Gwen, a scintillating boody-What's my duty? Tooti-fruiti au rooti -Shoobee doobee, who be you be? Scoobee doobee department of redundancy department! Stream of consciousness – What a long strange trip its bean-dip when you say that pardner! When Freud met Jerry Garcia Then Leah was heah (SIC) Be here now's da time!

My wife really likes to make pottery, but to me it's just kiln time.

I took my boat, "Pepper", out for a sail. When I returned to port, I rammed the pier and it ripped the side of the vessel. It was a sad day when the dock tore "Pepper".

Bonnie, music teacher, tough ass lookin' (kissy face, smokin-place)

Iguana is know chicken, Cantina, mellow lickin',
Guitara its a pickin', with Bonnie I am smitten!
Can't beat da Heights, just seed the sites,
Romantic nights just might be rite !
As time goes by, I find her captivatingly beautiful,
infatuatingly interesting, magnificently musical,
scintillatingly sensual, tremendously talented,
& alluringly alliterative. Watt an electric profile!
Eyes a sap for beauty, what's my duty?
where's my boody? tutti-fruiti, au-rooti, already!
Know iguana cantina wit Bonnie I iz dumped.
No fat, no sugar, no booze, no sex, no respect. I really get no respect, tiz a hex, don't get bumped, better to get pumped wit a jump on a rump then a hump on a chump!
Crumpets will trumpet my dumpedness.

Viagra is not Kosher for Passover. The argument is that it is coated with a leavening agent. Is that what makes it rise to the occasion?

If you take a laptop computer for a run, you could jog your memory.

Adrianne (Professor, 1999). I answered her ad in the Globe Personals & on our 1st date she had me pick her up at her apt. in Dorchester where we were meeting for the 1st time. I wore a sport jacket & she was appropriately dressed. We went out to eat on the Quincy Marina at a restaurant overlooking the water. It was lovely. I took her home & gave a little peck on the cheek & we said goodnite.

The next time, she invited me over to her place for dinner & she kissed me real good, this time & we were off. I would have to say, some of the best sex I've ever had, & she was older than me. She didn't want me to use a condom, which was fine by me. I thought I needed Viagra, but no longer with her. She was a left wing, Catholic activist – the left wing activist, I was fine with, but the religious Catholic, who wanted me to go to Church with her, I was not thrilled about! Plus, when I told her that I wouldn't consider marrying anyone who wasn't Jewish, she ended our relationship very soon thereafter. c'est la vie!

Rita was someone I met at a Video Dating Service. We didn't really click, but I wrote her a poem at first meeting:

silly Billy & filly Milly (quite a dilly) walked willy nilly, whilst marvy Harvey & sweeta Rita shared a pita, piece o' (de resistance) pizza, pleas to feed her, knead her feet, soar! Some sweet feat, lore (can't beat Keats!) core is pure! fore, just playin' around!

Rabbinical Sex Therapy:

An older Jewish gentleman marries a younger lady and they are very much in love. However, no matter what the husband does sexually, the woman never achieves orgasm. Since a Jewish wife is entitled to sexual pleasure, they decide to ask the rabbi. The rabbi listens to their story, strokes his beard, and makes the following suggestion:

"Hire a strapping young man. While the two of you are making love, have the young man wave a towel over you. That will help the wife fantasize and should bring on an orgasm." They go home and follow the rabbi's advice. They hire a handsome young man and he waves a towel over them as they make love. But it doesn't help and she is still unsatisfied. Perplexed, they go back to the rabbi. "Okay", says the rabbi, "let's try it reverse. Have the young man make love to your wife and you wave the towel over them."

Once again, they follow the rabbi's advice. The young man gets into bed with the wife and the husband waves the towel. The young man gets to work with great enthusiasm and the wife soon has an enormous, room-shaking, screaming orgasm. The husband smiles, looks at the young man and says to him triumphantly,...
"You see, THAT'S how you wave a towel!"

Does the name Pavlov ring a bell?

A successful diet is the triumph of mind over platter.

When you dream in color, it's a pigment of your imagination.

A gossip is someone with a great sense of rumor.

Without geometry, life is pointless.

> What happens if you throw a centigrade thermometer up in the air? It becomes fair in height.

CHONG Wrong "chose" me at GE video dating service. I called her, we made a date, which I postponed by calling her at the last minute, and scheduled the date for a week later. However, when I called her on the day of the date (the week later, 3 hours before the scheduled time), there was no answer, but I assumed <when you assume you make an ass of You & Me!> she would be at the pre-agreed place. It took me 2 hours to get there & I waited for another hour but she never showed. I called and left messages on her machine & sent her an E-mail. She finally called me back 3 days later & said that because I didn't call to confirm before the day of the date, she did something else! What a space shot. I told her she could come to me if she wanted to meet... Au Revoir!

here's her poem:

RING WRONG BONG/DING DONG CHONG WANG TO EWE SHEEPISH DUDE, MISS STEAK IF YUR A VEGETARIAN (SIC OR WATT?) LACTOSE FREE VEGAN OR MORE, CARNIVORE WHORE? THE POOR AT THE DOOR HAVE LORE FROM BEFORE ON THE FLOOR, AT THE FORE-FRONT OF CENTER NOT LEFT OR BEREFT JUST DEFTLY CLEFT FROM TEFLON, LEFT ON KITTY KORNER, DOG GONE IT, ALLRITE- I'VE DONE HADDOCK WIT CHU, NO CLUE, JUST FER DA HALIBUT -WIT BREW. A FEW (I KNEW) WERE BLUE FROM SKEW OF HUE WIT CUE OF DEW. WHO KNEW I WAS A JEW? TRUE BLUE, IMBUE US WIT WATTS HAPPENIN' AT DA ZOO – NU?
Two pence vents tents stolen four dense tense capital of-fence!

Bull diddle steers little. MOO, cows on dee udder hand,
give milky way of zen, when ten men show yen
for penny ante-dis-establish-mentarian-ism schizm!

Is a book on voyeurism a peeping tome?

Dancing cheek-to-cheek is really a form of floor play.

Banning the bra was a big flop.

Our bikinis are exciting. They are simply the tops.

Why was the patient annoyed by the witty surgeon?
Because she was always making cutting remarks.

Attilla (Physician/Witch) 2002 answered my Personal Ad in the Phoenix which read:

Attentive Lover: tall, SJM, 52, progressive, left-leaning, affectionate, & kind, loves jazz & blues, seeks good kisser for LTR.

She said she was a good kisser & wanted a LTR, so we met for tea at Carberry's, then met for dinner at Redbones, then I went to her home for the KISSFEST, 2 hours of intimate kissing, then dinner; & a month later I went over for a 4 hour MASSAGE-FEST plus dinner; then she broke up with me.

Here's the dear Harvey she wrote me:

Hi, Harvey...

I've been thinking and feeling about our time together, since the massage fest. On deep reflection, I am sorry to say, I am not in an emotional space right now to pursue further, deeper erotic connections...Even with the disclaimer about not going for a "heart connection" and your comfort with that, I am aware that I am not feeling enough of an erotic connection to move into more sex play, together...

I think that a lot of this is about where I am in coming out of my last relationship. I have recently ended sexual connections with two other men in my life (I am, by nature, a "polyamorous" person, something that we haven't talked about). That's my way of saying "Don't take this TOO personally". The truth is, I am feeling very a-sexual these days. I'm wondering if this is something to wait through and see if it passes. I choose not to, right now.

Even without my low libido, I am noticing that we don't have as much in common as I would hope, for good friendship-into-lovership. You are a good kisser, but it is "wetter" kissing than I like. You got freaked out by a lover "topping" you, and I just finished an exploration about a month ago with a man deeply into S&M, complete with collars, chains, and blindfold. I like to dance, and the places I go aren't that interesting to you (rightfully, with your diabetes you really need to protect your feet, and my "barefoot boogies" aren't appropriate). You love jazz, and I don't see myself hanging out comfortably at jazz clubs with a White guy...Been there. Done that.

Different strokes, definitely...Even on the Black/ Jewish thing, we seem to be at different ends of the spectrum. Imagine a black woman who doesn't know jazz!! And I sometimes attend Shabbats with friends who come from very progressive Shuls but you practice in a more(?) conservative (Sic) temple... (NOT TRUE!) So, this is my "Dear Harvey" letter. I hope that you proceed with other leads from your personal ad, and do well.

Poem fer Attilla

Which Doctor Attilla, the killer, diller, likes vanilla from her feller, well, I'll tell ya...What do Penn & Teller, Helen Keller, & Old Yeller's cellar have in common, do tell her? A Bell, quel kvell! (O-Hell is tent in Hebrew, intense oui brew a stew so few dey knew da cue for hue review, so do in lieu of ewe, a sheepish moo-cows on dee udder hand, can-do! No Bull should ever shoulder dat miss steak !

Audrey 2003

I signed up for free singles websites in Dec.2002. One of the websites had an additional free print newspaper personal so I let them write my ad for me:

> Tall, progressive, affectionate, kind, left-leaning, musical, SJM, 52, musician, writer. Seeks attractive, loving woman, 45-55, who's a good listener with a good sense of humor.

Audrey, a Scandinavian woman a few years older than me, answered the ad & we hit it off hot & heavy (tongue in cheek + throat) right off the bat. We fell in love with each other so quickly it must have been a physical infatuation cuz we were both lonely we had an intense affair for less than 2 months & then she let me know, 3 days before my birthday, that I was unacceptable to her cuz of my herbal habits – c'est la vie!

Here's my poems for Audrey –
1st Poem for AGM:

My tongue lusts for your loins,
licking your troubles away,
the clitoral truth is gently touching my heart,
such singing is bringing
me closer & closer to thee –

1/7/03

At one with the pear, we're a pair of dear,
here, there, & everywhere – a multiple, orgasmic fruit
instrument of love, hovering, fantastically above like elastic
loving doves – oui kneed each other's doe,
deer, hare here wit bare peer!...fondly, H. T. Rabbit, Hare

A Tonal Poem (ATP for AGM)

1/17/03

Dear Audrey, deer, Harvey, hare, here,
bare peer, preparing a pair of pears!
At one wit da pear – prepare loving lips –
oui lick a pair, here, there, & everywhere –
a multiple, orgasmic, luscious,
fruit instrument of love appears,
apparently, fantastically, hovering above
like elastic loving doves
(or iz dat stretchin two bits o' honey–)

revised 1/17/2003

aye, luv ewe! scoo-ba-ly, boo-ba-ly, Shoo-ba-ly-doo,
you-be, oui-be, Tee Hee be few,
dat knew da crew dat brew
da Basin street bruise
onto cues fer hues of true, blue,
I love youse! scoo-ba-ly-doo's to yuz too's Boo, Boo's,
bearing (baring) Hara el Conejo Yogananda T. Ra-beet!

REVILED 2/8/03

(dumped by AGM for my birthday!)
El Conejo, Missed Her Potato Head

At one wit da pare, food'l do-dat too ya, apparently appealing
a pair o' nuttin' honey-you're chokin'?!
Wry'd! Oh my Guinness! Oh ya Kid(ah)knee/
up your chim – a ney – formerly known as Sydney,
O feel ya-Will ya pleas?

Letters to me, my shelf & aye, me bucko

Is Isis, an Egyptian goddess?
Green with envy addressing Hamlet, I am bic.
2B-R knot 2B? Dat is da quest-shun + how long is a Leroy Blue?
Dear are dose dat are knot too tied up to pull the chain of
events transcending it all into a happening, sing, thing! Tra-
Ling-a ding -bring-fling, cling to zing wit ping king! Ring me
up! Scotty!

NUN PUN: Shirley, ewe jest —
its really a lyric limerick habit:
Do Nuns travel in pairs?
None dew or so it appears!
Two Nun's having fun,
were said , on the run,
its unsettling, all their affairs!

Count of Orange you glad we're Bach
to Basics or Kant you Handel, Hayden it?
Harvey T Rabid Hare (be gone) today, derrier & here
tomorrow, fair-care? Bare fare, where? Air! Please don't tear
dee rare, hare, hair, here, or we're where, we were, when we
were previously wearing worn wares, where neither here nor
there rather, we're dear, deer or sew, it appears!

UPSIDE RIGHT, DOWNSIDE LITE
LEFT SIDE BRIGHT, FLIP SIGHED SIGHT
JAZZ ME PLIGHT, TRANE DA BIRD
SWALLOW DEE MONK, DIZZY FOR MILES
BOBO AIN'T FATS, SLIM GOT COOKIN
HOOKED ON LEE-WARD OF LESTER LEAPING IN,
or iz dat OUT TO LUNCH WITH ERIC DOLPHY?

"The boppers flat their fifths.
We consume ours." – Eddie Condon

Right wry wringing wrongs relatively reluctantly regarding riots, all the while Ramon realistically reeks from paprika! Peek-a brew, icy hue, toodl-oo, to you, too, BooBoo – too few in lieu of true blue!

Please not too freaze fleas off the Sleaze,
take out the cheez, hold the peas, don't appease
or a sneeze. Seize the da-is. Table the motion, with a notion for a potion applying the lotion, so shun low, sweet Harriet, pummel forth to parry no groan! ET phone home! Joan moan shown! Bone, sown, drone, known, hone koan! hum-drum, one-some, fun, gummy bares awl! Imperialistic tool, capitalist fool, darn stubborn mule, inefficient fuels da fire it up! Numero Uno!

VACATIONS

Israel 1991 (Evi's Bat Mitzvah)

My cousin, who lives in Jerusalem, was having a Bat Mitzvah Party so I decided to visit for 3 weeks for a combination celebration of her Bat Mitzvah & a vacation for me. I stayed with my cousin Yaacov (the professor of Microbiology at Hebrew University who was the Bat Mitzvah girl's, Evi's, dad), and his family:his wife Ilana, & their other 2 kids, Shira & Doron. It was very nice to visit relatives in Israel & they showed me a good time. Then I went on a 4 day guided tour of the Sinai by jeep. It was great fun & I took a lot of pictures of camels, beduins, mountains & beach/desert scenes.

To win a relay race, swimmers pool their efforts.

Sydney, Australia R & R 1970

I went on Rest & Recuperation (R & R) leave for a week from Vietnam to Sydney, Australia in 1970. I went to a lot of clubs trying to pick up chicks or "birds," as they were known down under, but was on the whole unsuccessful until the last night that I was there. I was walkin down the street late, when I saw a couple of pretty girls with a guy who asked me if I was lookin' fer a bird. I said yes & he thrust this young Black chick into my arms dressed only in a fur coat. When I got her back to my hotel, I saw only her bra & panties on, under the coat which I quickly had off her but she was exhausted and was half asleep. I dunno if it was drugs or booz or both but I could only have sex with her so far. She was practically sleeping on me, then I had to leave the Hotel room at 6 AM & we didn't get to sleep until 3 or 4, so I woke her up & gave her all the Australian money I had left, about 5 dollars, & walked her out to the street. Toodaloo ...back to the Nam!

Amsterdam 2001

My 1st vacation in 10 years- I planned this a year in advance cuz I was taking care of my elderly Mom who couldn't be left alone for more than a day but my brother & his wife agreed to come & stay with our Mom for a week to let me go on vacation to Amsterdam, Netherlands-aka Holland! I got there after a direct flight from Boston's Logan Airport to Amsterdam's Schiphol Airport at 7:30AM. I took a train to the Central Station in Amsterdam Center and walked to my hotel, the INTEL, a real nice place but I couldn't check in until 3 PM.

They let me leave my luggage in storage, so I searched out my list of Coffee Shops and found my first one, the Rokerij. I was disappointed, but I didn't really know the scene too well, so I bought Delft China for presents & went looking for wooden shoes. I bought a few T-shirts in every coffee shop I went into. I had a shopping list of over 30 people. By the time 3 pm came around, I was exhausted, checked in, took a shower, a nap, & then I woke up and searched for more coffeeshops. I did some of the tourist stuff, like the Van Gogh Museum, the Portuguese Synagogue, The Trade Union Museum, the Red Lite District, etc.

Here's my Itinerary:

Amsterdam Aug. 6, 2001

<u>MON. 8/6/01</u> NWA/KLM-flt 38 going & flt 37 returning
Depart BOSTON, Logan @ 6:40PM 7hr. flt.
arrive amsterdam, Schiphol @ 7:35AM
<u>TUES. Aug. 7</u> Buy 35 post cards & stamps,
change money at <u>AMER.XPRESS – DAMRAK 66</u>
<u>MAIN PO/Singel 250</u>
<u>train to Central Station (20 min.)</u> restauratie on platform1
    (7am–10)
Go to GVB (Amsterdam Transport Authority) free tourist guidebook
    in <u>transit office</u>, – buy 5 day Dagkaart PASS
take tram #20A CIRCLE TRAM
<u>rijksmuseum vincent van gogh</u> – (10am-5pm) paulus potterstraat 7
<u>Stedelijk Museum of Mod. Art</u> – Paulus Potterstraat 13
    (11am–5pm)
<u>(3PM Thurs. & SAT – free concerts)</u>
<u>Heineken Brewery</u> – Stadhouderskade 78 (1PM 2hr. guided tour)
check in Hotel 3PM INNTEL, AMST. CTR. (Nieuwezijdskolk 19)
Casablanca-Zeedijk 26), red lite distr-free jazz bar (tu.&w.
    8PM–2AM)
<u>WED. Aug. 8</u> <u>THE OLD INDIAN HEAD SHOP, R.L.D.</u>
<u>PORTUGUESE ISRAELITISCHE Synagogue</u> (MR. Visserplein 3)
    (Sun–F 10am–4pm)
<u>BIMHUIS (Oude Schans 73–77)</u> **wed nite jam free**
th-sat. paid jazz @ 10:30PM
<u>Hash, Marij. & Hemp Museum</u>
(Oudezijds Achterburgwal 148) (11am–10pm)
<u>THURS. 8/9 **Jazz cafe alto**</u> (korte Leidsedwarsstradt 115)
(S-TH 9pm–3am, **free**)
<u>FRIDAY aug.10 **Bamboo Bar**</u> Lange Leidsedwarstraat 66
9pm-4am Thurs. **Fri.** Sat. **free**) (near Leidesplein)

FOOD:

HOI KING CHINESE (IE JAN Steenstraat 85) muntplein
Cafe Esprit in Spui Sq.
Rose's CANTINA — reguliersdwarsstraat 38-flow.mk
Nam Kee (11:30Am -midnite) Zeedijk 111-13
BOJO — near leidesplein(Lange Leidsedwarsstraat 51)
(m-w 4pm-2am; th-sun 12-2am)
New King (Zeedijk 117) red lite dist. (11am-12pm)
SUN. aug.12 check out of hotel by 12 noon — bus to airport
2:15PM — flight 37/NWA leaves Schiphol 8hr. flight
arrives at Boston, Logan at 4:05PM, Sunday Aug.12, 2001

Coffeeshops:

Grey Area C. S. (Oude Leliestraat 2) 12-9PM
    (between Dam Sq. & the Anne Frank House)
Homegrown Fantasy C.S. — (Nieuwe Zijds Voorburgwal 87a)
    (2 blocks nw of dam sq) 9am-12
BaBa (64 Warmoestraat — corner of Oudebrugsteeg — RLD)
Tweede Kamer (Heisteeg 6) 10am–1am (near the SPUI)
GreenHouse Centrum (Oudezijdes Voorburgwall 191)
    9am–1am (bet.Dam & Nieuwmark)
Greenhouse Namaste (Waterlooplein 345)
    9am–1am near MR Viss.
GREENHOUSE TOLSTRAAT Tolstraat 91(oud west-near overtoom)
    Sun-TH.10am-1am
DUTCH FLOWERS (Singel 387) near Spui (sun–thurs. 10am-1am)
Barney's Breakfast Bar (open 7am–10pm) Haarlemmerstraat 102
Kadinsky (Rosemarijnsteeg 9) 10am–1am near SPUI
Siberie (Brouwersgracht 11) 11am–11pm near Central
De Dampkring (Handboogstraat 29) 11am-1am near SPUI
Bluebird St. Antoniesbreestraat 71) (bet.Mr. Viss. & Nieuwmarkt)
    9:30am–1am
DeRokerij (Lange Leidsedwarsstraat 41) near Leidesplein 10–1am

ROKERIJJ 2 (Singel 8) near central train station 9am-1am
Betty Boop next to the INTEL HOTEL
GLOBAL CHILLAGE (Kerkstraat 51)
   off Leidsestraat near Leidesplein
KATSU – Eerste V/D Helststraat 70 (SOUTH)
Nes-Cafe – Nes 33 /Rusland – Rusland Straat 16
Andalucia – Halvemaansteeg 1 (Center East)
Cafe 420 De Kuil – Oudebrugsteeg 27
Kashmir Lounge – Jan Pieter Heijestraat 85

RADIO – FM 101.2 Classical & jazz after 10PM
Radio London-90.4 reggae, latin, & african
Wooden shoe factory – Nieuwe Hoogstraat 11– old ctr.os
Delft Earthenware for Bert, MA, Jude, A&D
Chocolates for Ma, Jude, & Naomi (+cheese)

$704.90 – NWA/KLM and 390 NLG/nite for INNTEL Hotel
as of jun 19, 2001 – booked

Anne Frank Huis(prinsengracht 263) 9am-7pm
American Embassy – 664–5661
ALBERT CUYP 67, Surinam & Chisnese food –
   open12 noon–10:30PM
ALBERT CUYP MARKT – albert cuypstraat (9am-4pm)
THE HEADSHOP (Kloveniersburgwal 39)
   east of dam sq. m-sat 11am-6pm
National Trade Union Museum (Vakbonds Museum)
   (Henri Polaklaan 9) t ram 9 to Plantage Kerklaan
   (tues–fri 11am–5pm, sat.1pm-5pm (near Mr. Viss.)
De Hoogte BAR (Nieuwe Hoogstraat 2a) m–th 10am–1am
Prostitution Info Ctr. Enge Kerksteeg 3
   @ the RL Dist. open-Tu/w/fri/sat 11:30am–7:30pm
Amsterdam Call Girls tel. 600–23–54

Hi BVM-ski!

Harv-ski here, do I dare to bare my hair,
no kneed to beware the fare as provided by
no fear, butt fare to lick, I mean two looks
at Dat Maiden Fair, no square! Watt a lewd, nude, skewed by
no feud, nor food, neither booed, nor boo hooed, brewed by
brood just too few'd, don't mean to bee rude, nor too crude,
just a dude!

a spaced oddyssey

PROPOSAL FOR BVM'S BASEMENT MUSIC STUDIO, SCHOOL & GALLERY

...Harvey T. Rabbit, presiding editorialist.
Initial Perspiration for INSPIRATION as ASPIRATION
(I prefer lokshun kugel to oodles of noodles or possibly
poodles without doodles on their cuticles) optimistic
pentameter would be nice, spice without lice nor fried fleas,
pleaz comply! Back to the notion, a potion for passion
percussive, rhythmic, tonal, not anal call and response, butt, a
preponderance of utterance without the talk! Don't gawk nor
balk unless ya sock it-oo-mee, scoobee doo-be,
shoo-be woobe, doobie, anyone?

Triple Entendre
(on tender tundra
wit-Barry & Harvey)

BVM AKA WEG-SKI

The Harvey Snap & The Barry Tap,
it's happenin' now!
It's finger pickin', pickle lickin',
prickly stickin', lokshun kugel.
Something, Nu?
Iz Ass-Kickin' sicken or stricken?
Strictly speakin' electric, watt chu say?
tickle me, freakin' quicken & peakin'!
Putt & pay'n pray & play, oy- veh!
The flow changes thru ethereal tubes of justice.
Just us must unite to fight the blight.
I'd rather take flight with a kite,
at some height, during bright, light, sight.
Fright? No Tanks! A Peace of da Sky, bye!

Verily Varicose in Vain, refrain!
Iz an oyster like a hip-ster
(stir fried bip-ster)
Or iz dat Shuster like a shoe store(horning in on brew-ska)
You, sir, are a rooster, or at least you usta,
Twist her? Mister? or iz dat her sister? Kissed her?
(after 9/11 frisked her, pissed her off/ missed the gist of the list)
Verily Varicose in Vain, refrain –
That bookends it!

2 beer or not too bare –
Our 4 bears: Yogi, Smokey, BooBoo & Grizzly,
having sore fears, tore pairs, warfares, & pore hairs)
including 4 Blahz, bah bah, black sheep,
plus scoo-ba-ly, doo-ba-ly doo, u.s.w.
blah, blah, blah – You can't get more blase than that,
unless its 4 bear ants (forbearance)!

Booty iz in the I of the Bee-holder,
especially a bear boody, barely...
HET phony baloney ain't Kosher
cuz if I am bic pentameter –
Tiz 5 ft. diameter, dam it or
Beaver Reliever, sushi deceiver,
Should we believe her?
Did you bone up, or did you phone OM?
I used the Telepotty to piss someone off-ity.
It flows like Uriah Heap's urinal velocity, verily bop-ditty!

FUN FACT # 96:
**When I was a doobee,
I usta bone up on da good stuff!**

RUMINATION MASTURBA-SHUN FUN FACT # 69:
**A pickle iz nuttin', honey, butt a cukumber/pulsation/
marination/exagerration/perturbation – zap,
yur crustacean!**

Elixir: What her dog does when she comes home.

Sign at a nudist camp: Sorry – Clothed for the winter.

A used car is not always what it's jacked up to be.

LEFT ALONE

**2 wrongs don't make a right but 3 lefts do!
– especially left wing, left-leaning, & left standing!**

Boody, KaKa, DooDoo & good ole #2:

DA BEAUTI- FIRE BURNS, WHILST
DA CRACK GARDENER SHINES ON.
SUNFLOWERS, SEEDED FROM THE PITS
OF PLUM-LIKE, PRUNE DANISH, FORMERLY
KNOWN AS PUMPKINSEEDS, CONCEDES DA FORMER RABID,
RAPIDLY RECURRING, REPETITIVE, JAZZ,
BLUES, & KLEZMER RABBIT!

THYME TWO SWING THE ZING THING!
SING A SONG OF ZINGERS,
TWO TO THE BUNCH,
PLAYING WITH YOUR ZINGER, SWINGS,
ITS MY HUNCH! SINGING WITH YOUR ZINGER
SEEMS THE THING TO DO
BOODY FIRE DOO DOO –
WATT ELECTRIC ZING DO BOODY DOO!?!

TO LOVE, TO FEED DA NEED FOR SEED
(MY WEED), SO HEED DA CREED OF BREED
DATS FREED FROM DEED OF DOO, INDEED
I DO, SO COO, SAYS EWE, SHEEPISHLY GRINNING
FROM EAR TO HEAR THE BEAUTIFIRE DO!
BYE... HARVEY T. RABBIT FORMERLY HARE,
NOW HAIR IS GONE, BUTT KNOT FORGOTTEN!!!

Da beatnik slouch...for wayne

no slouch, dat beatnik, he be 'round,
no square, but where can he be found?
or is it she dat make dat sound?
so sad to hear dat he be drownd,
so deep 'neath ocean, underground,
we weep, simpatico abound
& souls dey seep from every mound
a heap be I be mucho downed

ONE HUNG FULL MOON HOWL

wit Joanna Barry at da Wabbit-Cong
Sleight o' hand-out a site on the porch of such height, wit da torch,
bitter bite/Larry Spatz drooled on, rite? Spring me tie knee knots,
oh so tight, wast bisterical in flight movies:
DA-O rolls/out o' site- out of mined/Al hum bur ga-ga!
Was Boris's plea a better one? Ask Eenie's bro, a beduin!
Strip to the pearls, suck oysters, quick girls, nevermind Hong Kong,
what's wrong? Go westward Ho House! Time fer a change... and
the rabbits multiplied, dividing a multiplicity of arithmetic/
geometric hare hair here, barely bearing fair fare fearing division
incision subtracting the addition of a precision, revision, decision!

a tone poem epitome:

da tone tome tenshun poem, written whilst smitten,
no kitten at home, Hip iz hep'n, afore it happened-
hup toop treep trap-trippity dippity bippity bop,
re-bop shoo bam, yippi-kai-yay-go bop then scram-
sciddali, tiddali, piddali-jam, scoobaly, do-ba-ly
boob-aly scat, tiddli winkin at sounds like dat!

92

GONNIFF POINT PERMUTATIONS

No brewski here for Barry, there, be workski, where be kids,
butt hair, I screwski hare feel blowing care of windski bare no
engines, hear deze boats sail fair like kites in air, but Yogi bear,
eyes right, seea shellular notes on mares eat oats while doze y
dotes on little gone-if funny, grains of sunny songs, times up,
get lead out, oh so heavy debt. Must knead dough to make dee
bread, please feed the flow, now I must go cash in me woe is
we, Ma & PA, watt a kettle of fish we got me into!

2 wrists lite up da ship, pout mouths lie wit no lip,
artists try to add zip, but youths ain't always hip,
dats Nantucket US Lightship!

Yooz stuk wit me,
whoa baby can't chu see?
Dat wherever you may go
& whatever you may do,
I'z stuk wit chu,
like Elmer's GLUK,
unGLUK me glue,
oh babe, eyes stuck oui two,
cat forever purring,
oh sol mio, fa-mi-re-do.

Porgy, Bess loves you,
true lucky GLUK,
who's stuck you see,
oh maybe we all be,
sad endeavor screwey-poo,
Lucy, too! donchu few blink,
even blue, weg-ski, I's wit yu, like –
out Pearls suck (Boo Hoo).
Who knew a few, you too?

Re-cycling Back on Track
wit pack o'Tabac, no lack o'wanna
primarily Mary-wanna pot o' gold
to hold da fold of cold, fillet o' soul,
while bowling over tea.
Bold over...Chirpa,
grasping Ghatsby,
gasping sass-a-frass
whilst toking grass & kissing ass,
its a reel gas, round about midnite
at dat Jazz Brass Banned in Boss-town!
Boston baked, human beings
ovary, easy on the ayes have it!

adapt, adjust, survive, we must &
So its said, but why, I ask, is better,
best the truth, if not, forsooth, forsake us not,
cook the pot, don't be bought,
strive we ought, ideals we sought,
Reason rhymes with seasoned chimes.
Balance beam is off, is I'm?
NOW'S da TIME!

Did (Ja) here da one about the Jewish Woman who went to
her Orthodox Rabbi for advice regarding her upcoming
marriage? "Rabbi", she asked, "Is it permissible for me to
dance with my husband at our wedding?" "Absolutely not!",
responded the Rabbi. "OK", she says, "after we're married, is
it OK for us to make love regularly?" "By all means! Its a
Mitzvah (good deed)!"
"OK", says the Woman, "How about oral sex?" The Rabbi
responds: "Anything that is mutually agreeable, is permitted."
"How about me on top?" Again the Rabbi says: "Anything the
two of you wish to do is fine." "OK" she said, "How about
doing it standing up? "NO!" says the Rabbi, "That could lead
to dancing!"

Did you hear the one about the guy who fell into an incinerator... He made an ash of himself.

Did ya hair about the beatnik who had nothing to wear for the masquerade party so he sprayed his beard with deodorant & went as an armpit?

I was walking across a bridge one day, and I saw a man standing on the edge, about to jump off. I immediately ran over and said, "Stop! Don't do it!" "Why shouldn't I?" he said.
I said, "Well, there's so much to live for!"
"Like what?" "Well ... are you religious or atheist?"
"Religious." "Me too! Are you Christian or Jewish?"
"Christian." "Me too! Are you Catholic or Protestant?"
"Protestant."
"Me too! Are you Episcopalian or Baptist?"
"Baptist." "Wow! Me too! Are you Baptist Church of God or Baptist Church of the Lord?"
"Baptist Church of God." "Me too! Are you Original Baptist Church of God, or are you Reformed Baptist Church of God?" "Reformed Baptist Church of God."
"Incredible. Me too! Are you Reformed Baptist Church of God, reformation of 1879, or Reformed Baptist Church of God, reformation of 1915?"
"Reformed Baptist Church of God, reformation of 1915!" So then I said, "Die, heretic scum!" and pushed him off.

A young woman teacher explains to her class of children that she is an atheist. She asks her class if they are atheists too. Not really knowing what atheism is, but wanting to be like their teacher, their hands explode into the air like fleshy fireworks. There is, however, one exception.

A girl named Sara has not gone along with the crowd. The teacher asks her why she has decided to be different. "Because I'm not an atheist." "Then," asks the teacher, "what are you?" "I'm Jewish." The teacher is a little perturbed now, her face slightly red. She asks Sara why she is Jewish. "Well, I was brought up knowing and loving God. My Mom is Jewish, and my Dad is Jewish, so I am Jewish." The teacher is now angry. "That's no reason," she says loudly. "What if your Mom was a moron, and your dad was a moron. What would you be then?" A pause, and a smile. "Then," says Sara, "I'd be an atheist."

Pat is not feeling very well and he decides to go to a doctor. While he is waiting in the doctor's reception room, a nun comes out of the doctor's office. She looks very ashen, drawn and haggard. Pat goes into the doctor's office and says to the doctor: "I just saw a nun leaving who looked absolutely terrible. I have never seen a woman look worse." The doctor says: "I just told her that she is pregnant." Pat exclaims: "Oh my, is she?" The doctor responds: "No, but it sure cured her hiccups."

All of Santa's helpers are subordinate clauses

The moon in june stays mainly on the prune,
or how to run your mouth,
take care of bizness,
& spice up your life,
all at the same thyme.

Be Sage... Bee Pollen...
catch a falling star,
Putt paprika in your pocket,
save the gulf the gap the bridge the refrain from pain-strain to
remain sane then Cain will be able to be here now-
peace now and how, gee, wow!

Can a lune croon a tune on a dune as a boon
for Le Jeune at high noon and soon?
Peanut butter changes da flow,
while masturbatory glances obsess,
rationalization enters da stream,
only to heighten further disappointment,
continued disenchantment,
jaded dis-illusionment,
cynical, even futilistic,
pugilistic, semi-expected,
apathetic, Blah...

Did you see in the news last week about how little
money Dick Cheney gives to charity? In contrast, it was
just revealed that Joe Lieberman is the most charitable
member of Congress. He gives his entire paycheck to
Hadassah.

MILLION DOLLAR GIVEAWAY, WHEN I WIN THE LOTTERY ...

SPNI
Jean Towers
Naomi Moran
Richard & Judy Towers
Roberta Shulsinger
Barry Levenbaum
Randi Levenbaum
Rachel Cole
Karin Towers
Adrienne McDonald
Ruth Lederman & Tim Heeren
Sussanah Sirkin & Larry
  Harmon
Lenny & Carol Markowitz
Mark & Jan Green
Sylvia Medalie
Theresa Thompson
Rabbi Barbara Penzner
Norman Shore
Weezie Elses
Chas McCann
Len & Chao Ping Moss
David Jerome & Denise
  Delorey
Martha Brier
Mark Irwin
Dr. Jim Demicco
Henry Barber
Toby & Joe Dolph
Richard Cohen
Arthur Stepner
Steve & Nancy Kellerman
Eric & Helene Mishara
Alan Alpert

John Gibbons
Dr. Richard Shea
Shira Yashphe
David Slawsby
Barry Miller
Chaia Mide
Judith Antonelli
Eileen Feldman
Nancy & Fred Gadon
Susan Rosenberg/Jones
Billy & Janet Rosenberg
Dave Harris & Mimi Rabson
Toby Gutwill
Alan Hoffman
Julio Patino
Leah Patino
Ben Freiberg
Rosalie Gerut
Betty Silberman
Glenn Dickson
Magen David Adom
Joanne & Jim Conlin
John Michael Serkess
Lynn & Norman Foster
Hillel B'nai Torah
Mark Leonard
Cheryl Gagne
Lucia Grochowska-Littlefield
Rabbi Daniel & Hannah
  Tifferet Siegel
Special Needs Department @
  JCC- Newton
Janis Coulter Memorial Fund -
  A.F.H.U.

NOT MINE but – Wow are these bad...

1. Two vultures board an airplane, each carrying two dead raccoons. The stewardess looks at them and says, "I'm sorry, gentlemen, only one carrion allowed per passenger."

2. Did you hear that NASA recently put a bunch of Holsteins into low earth orbit? They called it the herd shot 'round the world.

3. Two boll weevils grew up in South Carolina. One went to Hollywood and became a famous actor. The other stayed behind in the cotton fields and never amounted to much. The second one, naturally, became known as the lesser of two weevils.

4. Two Eskimos sitting in a kayak were chilly, but when they lit a fire in the craft, it sank, proving once again that you can't have your kayak and heat it, too.

5. A three legged dog limps into a saloon in the Old West. He slides up to the bar and announces: "I'm looking for the man who shot my paw."

6. Did you hear about the Buddhist who refused Novocaine during a root canal? He wanted to transcend dental medication.

7. A group of chess enthusiasts checked into a hotel and were standing in the lobby discussing their recent tournament victories. After about an hour, the manager came out of the office and asked them to disperse. "But why?" they asked, as they moved off. "Because," he said, "I can't stand chess nuts boasting in an open foyer."

8. A woman has twins, and gives them up for adoption. One of them goes to a family in Egypt and is named "Amal." The other goes to a family in Spain; they name him "Juan." Years later, Juan sends a picture of himself to his birth mother. Upon receiving the picture, she tells her husband that she wishes she also had a picture of Amal. Her husband responds, "They're twins! If you've seen Juan, you've seen Amal."

9. These friars were behind on their belfry payments, so they opened up a small florist shop to raise funds. Since everyone liked to buy flowers from the men of God, a rival florist across town thought the competition was unfair. He asked the good fathers to close down, but they would not. He went back and begged the friars to close. They ignored him. So, the rival florist hired Hugh MacTaggart, the roughest and most vicious thug in town to "persuade" them to close. Hugh beat up the friars and trashed their store, saying he'd be back if they didn't close up shop. Terrified they did so, thereby proving that: Hugh, and only Hugh, can prevent florist friars.

10. And finally, there was a man who sent ten different puns to friends, in the hope that at least one of the puns would make them laugh. Unfortunately, no pun in ten did.

A good pun is its own reword.
I wished the buck stopped here, as I could use a few
Who stopped the payment on my reality check?
Madness takes its toll – Please have exact change.
Change is inevitable, except in vending machines.
Time flies like an arrow. Fruit flies like a banana!
What might you say to tell the cows and sheep
it is time to sleep? It's pasture bedtime...

Yur goin' thru yur stages,
just keep in mind dat sages
are finite unlike pages
that can transcend dee ages,
but meanwhile where's dee wages?

Reflexively rubber banned in Boss Town-
elastically fantastic, flexibly flyin', pleasingly plump it up-
pullet, tie one on, Taiwan Thai Juan, butt knot furlong,
horsin' around da bend of reality(Israel Tea) Chai
creed/bold breed/cold keyed up, droll deed eye dew, fold
freed from few, gold greed with goo, glue, hold heed of
hue, culled kri-yah, cued up, lulled leeward of mulled mead
lux lewis, lead, null need, no new pull, peed us off-ity,
bipity, bop-ity, rebop-a reel read (a real reed-a -boni-poni-
skoni-doodle crony-noodle-roni) only, bird-be-bop-eroni, do
stop da sullen seed, tz'all teed off the wall weed, y'all?

NORML-ize it!

Two Texans were seated at the end of a bar when a
young lady seated a few stools up began to choke on a
piece of hamburger. She was turning blue and obviously
in serious respiratory distress. One Texan said to the
other, "That there gal is having a bad time!" The other
agreed and said, "Think we should go help?" "You bet,"
said the first, and with that he ran over and said, "Can
you breathe??" She shook her head no. He said, "Can
you speak??" She again shook her head no. With that, he
pulled up her skirt and licked her on the butt. So shocked
was the young woman that she coughed up the
obstruction and began to breathe, with great relief.
Returning to his friend, the Texan said "Funny how that
hind lick maneuver always works."

What's left?

A MASS STATE OF CONFUSION:

The State of Texas, under the leadership
of Gov. George W. Bush, was ranked:

50th in spending for teachers' salaries,
49th in spending on the environment,
48th in per-capita funding for public health,
47th in delivery of social services,
42nd in child-support collections,
41st in per-capita spending on public education and...

5th in % of population living in poverty –

Also ranked:

1st in air & water pollution,
1st in % of poor working parents w/o insurance,
1st in % of children without health insurance,
1st in executions
(avg. 1 every 2 weeks for Bush's 5 years)

Just think of what he could do for US –
if he were *(elected)* president...

"Don't tell my mother I'm in politics; she thinks I play
piano in a whorehouse..."

"He played like he was in jail, behind a few bars and
couldn't find the key..."

BUSH IS FULL OF BEANS

The elect-shun is a tossup!
Does Gore have a Bush, or
will Bush Gore a hole in it?
    – its Nader here nor dear.

Even as
President Bush
tried during his
State of the Union
address on
Tuesday, January
28, 2003, to
convince
Americans that
war with Iraq
might be
unavoidable,

What's the count?

poets around the world were engaged in creative projects
for peace.

On January 19, Sam Hamill, the founding editor of Copper
Canyon Press, emailed an open letter to a few poets asking them
to "speak up for the conscience of our country" and add their
names to a petition against the proposed war with Iraq. Hamill
was responding to an invitation he received from First Lady Laura
Bush for a reception and symposium on "Poetry and the American
Voice" at the White House on February 12. Hamill decided to
compile the petition with a collection of anti-war poetry
(poetsagainstthewar.org) and present the anthology to Bush on
February 12 as part of A Day of Poetry Against the War. The
idea caught on: In just days he received nearly 2,000
submissions for the anthology, including work from Galway
Kinnell, Gregory Orr, Marilyn Hacker, John Balaban, Ursula K. Le
Guin, and Adrienne Rich.

At the end of January, First Lady Laura Bush indefinitely
postponed her symposium and reception, "Poetry and the
American Voice," after many of the nation's finest poets declined
her invitation in order to protest the war. Since then, *Poets Against*
***the War* has made significant progress in rallying opposition to**
the Bush administration's planned assault on Iraq.

POETS AGAINST THE WAR

poem submission on 2/5/03
by Harvey T. Rabbit

WORLD TRADE TOWERS OVER INJUSTICE,
BUSH TURNS UDDER CHEEK ON
SYSTEMIC CAUSES PENTAGONAL WASTE –
SENSELESS CIVILIAN DISASTER
IS A WAKE UP CALL TO VIGILANCE –
ETERNAL VIGILANCE IS
THE PRICE OF FREEDOM –
LOVE IS THE ONLY FREEDOM
IN THE WORLD.
LOVE IS THE PATH,
PEACE IS THE WAY
THAT WAS ZEN, then
THIS IS TAO, now

don't be irate – I ran a rack of hate,
not gater-fraid but grate on fate of da late, great
rate of refus-nik unabated train of thought process,
conscious awareness, Peace! Center!
Need pow wow & how…Peace Now!

WAR-ITS NO CHOKE (JOKE)!

April 1, 2003

Peace, Soon?

All war-ed out cut the cleaver, ward
before must needs poor folk-get cored!
stress relief, bas relief, trees re-leaf
whine not, grief be brief where's da be-fore
da war negotia-shuns?

A letter with a yellow rib on to logical
ties lighten up-no oil-tanx a bunch fer da crunch.
My hunch-no bunch a munch o' punch
& Judy in da skies (Lucy in disguise) –
sizin' up a peace of da pies!

Betty's apples 'n orange ya glad bannanas are appealing?
Date a fig – be a fruit, prune a twig, 'ease a beaut!
Who'z-itz newt or a futile burning bush! Stolen elections/anti
selections/appease a tease
seize the dais, table the motion, apply a lotion,
got a notion to cross da ocean,
sew wit out needles, shun low sweet harriet –
pummel forth to carry no moans
– no more more war nor groans,
just hone doze koans for peaceful tones in poems.

> A farmer brought his daughter a pet pig, which she called Frisky whenever it was in her room, and Ballpoint whenever it was in the sty. He asked her, "Why do you have two names for your pig?" She replied, "Ballpoint is just his pen name."

Harvey T. Rabbit

EDUCATION

University of Massachusetts, Amherst
BA in psychology 1986
Berklee College of Music, Boston
60 cr. in audio recording/music 1973, '79–82
Hebrew College, Brookline
Judaic Studies & ULPAN 1989–1995
Meah Program 2003
Hebrew University, Jerusalem
Hebrew language studies 1977
Boston Latin School – Diploma 1967
National Honor Society
Newton Cable Access TV (NCAC)
Production program 1996

RADIO EXPERIENCE

WMFO, Tufts University/Medford, 1979–86, 1990
Jazz D.J.: *Just Jazz, Radio Free Jazz, Jazz Variations, The Morning After Blues, Freeform Radio,* & *Classical Variance*
Producer & host of weekly live concert show: *On the Town*
Board operator, Engineering & Operations Assistant, Production Manager & Technical Teacher

WNTN, Newton Israel Radio Hour 1979

WMUA, Amherst – UMASS Jubilation in Jazz 1976

THEATER EXPERIENCE

Producer & Sound:
KLEZFEST & *Nite of Eclectic Music* – Temple Hillel B'nai Torah, West Roxbury, 1989–'92, '94–'95, '99–2003

Stage Crew:
Berklee Performance Center, Boston, 1979–'82

Spot light operator: *Dancin' in the Streets* – Next Move Theater, Boston, 1981

Sound: *Lies My Father Told Me* – Jewish Theater of New England, Newton, 1987

MUSICIAN/PERFORMER

Bass & Tenor Trombone:
Studied w/Roland Young, 1963–'65
John Coffee, 1965–'67
Larry Weed, 1967–'68
Ben Elkins, 1980–'81
Dave Harris (Overture & Pro Tools Free), 1999–'03
Barry Miller (Free Style Improv), 1982–'84
Boston Latin School Orchestras, 1963
UMASS Symphony & Marching Bands, 1967–'68
Amherst Jazz Orchestra, 1967–'68
The Berklee College POPS & Basie Swing Orchestras, 1979–'81
JCC Klezmer Band, 1985–2000
Tunefoolery, 1995–2001
Klozet Klezmer, 1989–1994
Klezmerific Quintet, 2001–'02
ongoing ensembles, concerts, and jams

Piano:
Studied w/ Fay Cipriano, 1959–'60
Ray Santizi, 1973, '79

OTHER EMPLOYMENT

Shammas (Sexton)@Temple HBT 2001–03

Special Needs Asst@JCC, Newton 1999–'01

Media technician@Instructional Resource Center, Sargent College, Boston University. 1991–'93

Interviewer@B.U. Center for Psychiatric Rehabilitation 1990

Rural Carrier@US Postal Service 1988–90

School Bus Driver@Arnold Transport 1978–'79, '81–'82

Taxi-cab driver@Boston Cab 1975

Day Care teacher@Central School 1983–'84

Resident/Worker on Israeli Kibbutzim '73–'74, '77

Hotel Desk Clerk@Kings Hotel, Jerusalem '76–'77

V.I.S.T.A. Volunteer@Belchertown State School 1971–'72

MILITARY SERVICE

Sgt. E-5, USMC(MOS-3041) Supply Administration
1969–70 Vietnam Tour – Honorable Discharge

INTERESTS

Music, stamp collecting, offbeat poetry, aesthethics, massage, Jewish mysticism, science fiction, ethics, social justice, peace

About the Author:

Harvey T. Rabbit,
53, is a 6'2" tall, offbeat poet &
Ex-Marine veteran of Vietnam,
with a BA in psychology from
University of Massachusetts,
several years at Berklee College of Music in Boston,
studying audio recording, trombone & piano;
and miscellaneous world experience –
from Woodstock to Jerusalem!

Rabbit Enterprises

Publishing Books & Music CD's

Musician Referral

Basement Recording Studio

359 Corey Street, West Roxbury, MA 02132 USA

email: HTRabbit@aol.com   www.RabbitEnterprises.US

toll free: 1-866-263-3983 + Pin# 5320

COUPON for ordering

RABBIT DROPPINGS:
The Autobiography of a Wabbit... by H. T. Rabbit
includes CD of Improvisational Music & Poetry

US $29.95 (MA residents add 5% sales tax, $1.50)
<u>FREE SHIPPING in US</u>

Credit Card #_____exp. date:_____

Signature:_____

Name:_____

Address:_____

City:_____State:_____ZIP:_____

Tel.#:_____

e-mail:_____

QTY._____@ $29.95 ea _____

Mass residents add 5% sales tax @ $1.50 ea _____

TOTAL _____

Please make checks payable to: Rabbit Enterprises & mail to:

Rabbit Enterprises
359 Corey Street
West Roxbury, MA 02132 USA

Toll Free 1-866-263-3983 + Pin# 5320
email: HTRabbit@aol.com
www.RabbitDroppings.com   www.RabbitEnterprises.US